# All the Work I Never Wanted:

## A Memoirella of Jobs

## by Rex Marshall

Library of Congress
Paperback ISBN: 979-8-9913071-7-8
Ebook ISBN: 979-8-9913071-8-5

Book Team:

*Production and Managing Editor: Michelle Kicherer*
*Book design and proofing by Gwendolyn Schulte at*
*GRS Editorial, LLC*
*Cover art by Justin Gradin*

*This is a work of nonfiction. That said, names and identifying
features have been changed to protect people's identities.*

Banana Pitch Press
bananapitch.com

*This book is dedicated to all the corporations who I've given about four decades of my life to. Thanks for the minimum of wages. And the 15 minute breaks—just the perfect amount of time to wipe away the tears and feel refreshed.*

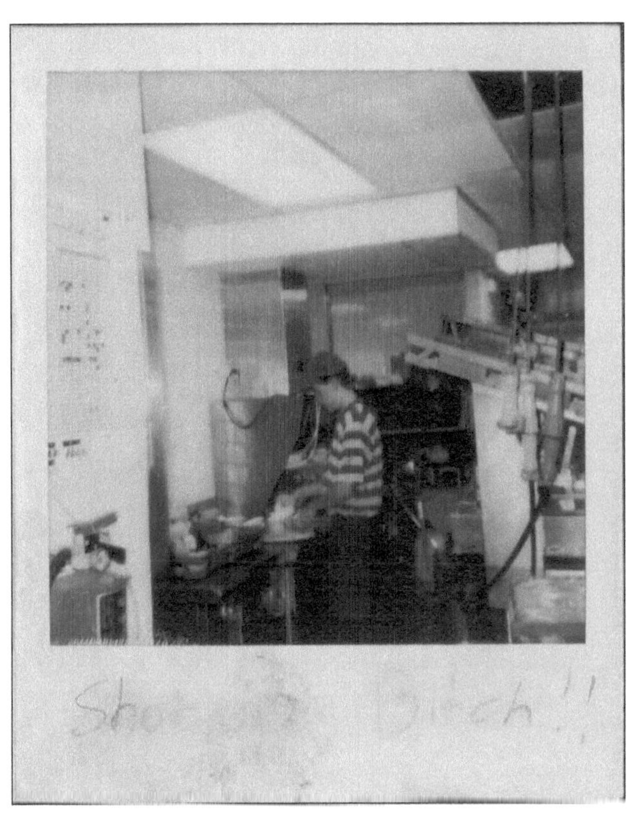

One night after my shift at the Holiday Inn, I took off my uniform pants (the cheapest black dress pants I could thrift) and there on my right leg was an oval of skin where no hair was growing. Did I shave a circle on my leg while I was asleep? Are there medical journal papers about Sleep Shavers? I touched the bare spot. My mind raced with conspiracy theories and conjecture. I looked in the mirror again. The hair on my head was fine. I was a bellboy, twenty-two and somehow surviving. Avoiding coworkers and dodging chores were the stressful parts of this job. Jobsite thoughts were: Where was I going to hide and read my paperback? Can I shut off this walkie-talkie and not get in trouble? Did I make enough coffee for the lobby?

Something radioactive? I did pick up treasures off the streets and put them in my pockets. Pockets! Keys! I carried a girthy ring of keys for every single door in the hotel. Had them in my right pocket. My bald leg spot was on my right leg. Where the keys swished in my pocket. Eight hours a day, four days a week of key ring rub rub rub. I was being ground down by a key ring. How many pocket rubs till it broke through my skin and infected my leg? A few years? Enough time to custom-whittle a peg?

In ninth grade we had mandatory meetings with the school counselor. The counselor's role was murky. He was supposed to be someone to talk to. He wore a sweater vest and a trained smile. Had a limp mustache. He was curt, bored, and had 1,100 kids to guide into the future. I don't think he was cruel, but his impatience was chewable. He was usually overrun by the truly unruly kids we had. One kid that kept bringing knives. A girl that was always drunk. Gang members. I never saw the counselor until I was forced to. To have a chat about college. I was a B student with no enthusiasm. I loved writing, I loved reading, and that was that. I had no feeling of destiny or knowing what I was born to do. I wanted college because that's what everyone else wanted. It kinda sounded like if you didn't you were a complete loser.

"What do you want to be?" the counselor asked.

"I have no idea why I was born," is what I should have said. What I did say: "I would like to maybe be an astronaut. But archaeology is good too." I shrugged. I had fantasies about being Indiana Jones. Digging up Tyrannosaurus bones. The Challenger explosion had pretty much blown up my interest in being an astronaut.

"Welllllll, those take a lot of college. Not everyone is right for college, you know. You have to be the best to get there. What about a custodian? I think you would be great with that. Or sanitation. It's a fine job with decent pay and you wouldn't have to do all the hard work of college. That's what I see for you, Rex. Maybe construction. But probably custodian or a warehouse. Fine jobs, really."

I left his office with dark questions cursing my brain. That guy thinks I'm a garbage man. I looked at my clothes. I had a growth spurt and my pants were about two inches above my ankle. My sneakers were held together with duct tape. My Kmart Rustler denim made me low class for sure. I had no extracurricular activities. I had no secret skills or savant hints. I thought I was smart but maybe I was destined for the dump.

My Grampa reveled in his tales of the golden days when a factory machine sucked his hand into a spinning gear and turned it into hamburger. They put it back together, he went back to work and made forty-one years at the Owens Bottle Factory. The lady training me at the plastic factory in Jean, Nevada was missing fingers. We worked on what could have been the very machine that clipped them off her hand. "Don't reach up under this area, because, well, see here?!" And she waved her chopped hand and grinned.

Here's a fantastic, enthralling, hardly-embellished written account of my job history from 1987–2002. All the work I never wanted. I can retire in about nine years, or so my HR department says. A close-to-seventy-year-old coworker recently and heavily said, "You can never save enough money to retire. It will never be enough." I felt guilty buying my lunch that day for sure.

May you and I never have another job again. Vote for the person who says No New Jobs! No job creation on my watch! My time got me $3.75 an hour when I started. Thirty-five years later and I'm up to $31.46. That's better. Is that better? That's better. It's only my life. We've got to pay till we die. Probably work until we die, too. That's depressing. Whoops. Live laugh cheat on your taxes, take long lunches, use all your sick days, come in late and leave as early as you can, comrades. Timeclocks are forever. Don't forget your fifteen minute break.

# Las Vegas Review Journal

1987–88
$0/HOUR

I had breakfast while watching Johnny Carson. Corn Pops, Fruity Pebbles, or Sugar Smacks. I listened to the jokes, made note of when my Dad laughed. He sat in a billowy La-Z-Boy, his legs folded in a warped "Indian style," as we used to say. He drank Folgers, smoked generic cigarettes, and stubbed out the dead ones in a giant conch shell on the coffee table. It was 11 p.m. and I was twelve. My Mom would wake me by having our cocker spaniel Mindy jump on my bed. The overhead burned my eyes but it was a tender way to get woken up.

The streetlights in Las Vegas were orange. High-pressure sodium bulbs. Each one created a zone of candle light ambiance. The pattern was hypnotic. Small spheres of unnatural pulsing color as we buzzed down Interstate 15. Dad and I drove straight into the neon, which from our house, way south in the desert, was a glow on the horizon. Like a sun that wouldn't set. Like headlights that never made it over the hill. Dad smoked, the ash blew around the van. I stared out the window feeling devious. The night time was taboo. I was in the forbidden zone.

We sat in the van and waited to be called up. Sometimes it took hours. A dozen busted, dented, rattly, coughing old vans and trucks sat in the lot of the *Las Vegas Review Journal,* the city's largest paper. A guy would walk out on the dock and shout your name loud. When your district was called, you backed up to a conveyor belt and the newspapers rolled out in bundles. It was backbreaking, loading bundles of paper, stacking them like a ceiling-high puzzle in the van. Stacking until the van would be grinding the street as we drove away. Sparks on speed bumps.

The printing press broke all the time. Dad would cuss, slam the door of the van. I'd watch him go into the printing building, waving his arms high. It was too easy to read his lips. He'd come back. "Well you better like waiting," he'd say at me. "Don't start whining about it."

I never whined about it.

One night, Dad threw a paperback in my lap. "Did you read this yet?" It was a sci-fi I had never heard of. Larry Niven. I would usually finish a book in a week. "Did you finish it? Okay, do this one now." Robert Heinlein. Philip José Farmer. I read fast and tried not to scuff the covers. He never asked me about them and I never talked about them.

Some nights he would talk at me, give me the lay of the land.

"Never trust a woman, kid. Look at your goddamn mother. She's a fat pig. I pay for everything and I'm out here seven nights a week and she got fat and bitches. That's what a woman will do if you let them. You think I want to come home to a fat pig? It's my fucking money."

"Now, holy shit, look at the lungs on that one!" he said on a different night as a woman walked across the street from where we parked. "That's a piece of trim! Fuckin' A." I bring this one up only because I thought for a while that boobs might actually help women breathe. Are they full of air? Do they deflate?

I guess that is a bit of obnoxious writing. But this was part of the job for me: listening to an angry man trapped in a shitty job. These graveyard shifts turned out to be the most time I would ever spend with this stranger called Dad. It was not what you would call quality time. This is dramatic talk but I think I probably have a pinch of brain damage from working graveyard as a developing child. I was already a daydreaming kid who could stare out the window for hours. Graveyard shift made it worse. Everything felt like a dream. My mind was a kite flying high while my dumb hand was ground level holding the string as I gazed into an anthill. Everything blurs when you are active in the sleep zone. My eleventh and twelfth summers were spent as a zombie chucking newspapers into the dead of night. I was an underpaid ghost haunting the neon-splattered graveyard shift.

Wednesdays were coupon days and Sundays had the funnies and pages of coupons. Those were the biggest, fattest newspapers. I feared those days. Rubber bands snapped on my hands trying to fold those giant burritos. Those two nights were the beasts. A bundle of Sundays probably weighed twenty-five pounds. Dad made me load the van on a Sunday on my own once. Trying to toughen me up I suppose. "Ok, start behind the driver's seat. Drop. Then you make a row to the right. Then behind that again on the driver's.

Then you go high, start the second high row on the driver's side. Then you lay another bottom row. It's like laying brick. Keep it tight! Or they will all come crashing down and crush us up front. Come on come on you gotta move faster!"

The conveyor belt was halfway in the van. I grabbed and chucked bails of newspapers over and over until my back was hard and stiff. My arms were jelly. It took about an hour to load on the heavy days. Dad jumped out to let some air out of the tires so they wouldn't pop. He hopped back in smoking and pointing where to stack. "There ya go, that hurts don't it? Hahaha!" He laughed. An hour into it I could barely jump out of the van. I crawled into the front seat. My back felt like concrete. My hands were raw and cracked, the bleeding stopped by black newsprint ink. The night had just begun.

We dropped the papers at the parking lot of the Terrible Herbst Car Wash on Sahara and Jones. The paperboys met us there. The paperboys were not boys but men, the youngest probably thirty-five. Most of the men and their vehicles were past their prime, beat up, stained black with newsprint. Drinking cheap and eating cheap and complaining. These guys couldn't hold regular jobs and so the graveyard shift paper game sucked them in. The oldest guy must have been in his sixties. Named Harold, I think. He drove a long cream-yellow Cadillac, the white leather interior ruined from news ink and eating fast food while driving. He foamed at the mouth when he talked, always had a scheme. Dwayne drove a leaky blue Dodge Ram, and one of his legs was deformed from polio. He was a nice guy and had gone to prison. Nothing violent but still an ex-con. He was stuck in low-wage orbit in a van that leaked every fluid you could name.

James was the champion. My Dad's star paper carrier. He was a quiet Asian kid with a gold Toyota pickup. He was going to UNLV, needed cash, and the graveyard worked with his class schedule. He could deliver 900 papers in four hours. "He must throw them like one a fucking second. It's unreal. And Harold over there, he wants more papers, but I give him four hundred and he gets five or six complaints a night and then I gotta go rethrow his route," my Dad griped.

James didn't show one night. Dad cussed but I could tell he was surprised and a little hurt. We had to deliver James's route that night. Papers should be at people's doors before the sun comes up. We started at midnight and didn't get home till 11 a.m. I folded and rubber-banded over a thousand papers. I lost my mind with how many papers there were. It was the longest night of my life to that point. I was tired and soon that tired was overtaken by a bigger tired, and the next tired, which I thought was all I could take, became a new and improved tired. Etc. etc. till sunrise, till 10:30 when McDonald's served breakfast and my Dad treated me to the best Ultimate Sausage McMuffin and Egg I had ever had.

James didn't show the next night or any other. The news piece was in the Saturday paper. James had been traveling at high speed on Blue Diamond Highway when he lost control of his vehicle. The pictures showed the burnt-out crumbling black-metal carcass of his gold Toyota. Part of it had melted into the asphalt with the heat of the flames.

"The kid didn't even drink. I didn't know he was epileptic, Jesus fucking Christ. Poor motherfucker. I'll have to hire two people to replace him, that's what really burns," said Dad.

Staring at the photos, I imagined driving fast and losing control. Not being able to move and feeling the Toyota drift, slip off the road. Being paralyzed as it flipped and tumbled and watching the flames burst from the hood. Or maybe being lucky enough to be unconscious.

We split James's route up that night. Me and Dad delivered 400 of the papers, someone else took the other 400. I folded the newspaper with those pictures of the end of James, wrapped the local section with the rest of the Saturday edition. Learning how to fold a paper takes practice. There is a right way to make a crease, a best angle to come over the top with a rubber band. By the end of this infinite night I was a pro. We drove through apartment complexes, track home cul-de-sacs, endless strip malls; hacking at those paper routes for hours, throwing the paper with James's page out the van window over and over and over until the sun came up.

One time, the guy with the polio limp stood up for me. My Dad was calling me a dipshit. A lot of times he would tell me to do something without showing how to do it, and get angry when I didn't know how to do it. "Check the oil in the van, Jesus fucking Christ! Are you slow? Is it leaking oil or not? Do I have to do all this shit myself 'cause I have a dipshit son?" Dad ranted. Dwayne stepped in.

"Hey Richard, come on man. He's just a kid. He doesn't have a car, boss. I'll show him how to do it, but you know this thing is always leaking just like my piece of shit." And Dwayne showed me how to not make my Dad angry on that front, showed me the dipstick and all that. He ruffed up my hair in a way that made me feel sad but comfortable.

Vegas is a city that never sleeps. Vegas has a night city and a day city. The two rarely meet. Graveyard folks wake up at 8 or 9 p.m., go to work at 11 and are home by 8 a.m. There are cars on the streets at all hours. Most places are open 24/7. Even away from the Strip and Downtown you have people grocery shopping at 2 a.m. Eating dinners at 4 a.m. You could walk into a casino, or even a bar, and not leave for days.

We delivered the paper to a bank building. The old security guard was there every night to chat. My Dad would usually park the van and tell me to wait. The guard would let him in the building and he'd come out maybe thirty minutes later. I'm positive they were drinking while talking shit. One of those nights the routine didn't go as usual. My Dad was back in less than fifteen minutes looking pale.

"Charlie wasn't in. They said he died. He died right here while on the job. Last night. After I delivered the paper. They said he lanced a boil on his leg with a pocketknife and bled out. What the fuck. It must've been quick. He didn't make it to call an ambulance and they found him when they opened. Jesus."

I didn't have anything to say. I was eleven or twelve and had never heard of such a goddamn thing. I imagined the scene and how terrible it must have been to be that guy. Spending his final moments like that. Also, how bored at work do you have to be to start stabbing yourself with a knife? I imagined the morning coworker who started their day off by finding that gory scene. Work mornings are bad enough.

When my Dad first drafted me, I was promised minimum wage. $3.50 an hour I think. I did two summers and saw no cash. My Dad was pissed whenever I had to go back to school. I felt relief about not working graveyard, but was exhausted thinking about school life. I would have to figure out how to be around a mass of kids again. And transition into daywalker life. Fall came around and my parents seemed to have forgotten my birthday. Nothing happened on my birthday, anyway. A few days after, my Dad dropped a huge box next to me on the couch. "Here, it's the Nintendo. Don't say I never gave you anything. I never had this when I was a kid." And my Mom completed the gesture: "We paid for that out of the money your Dad owed you for working. 'Cause we are trying to get ahead and you can't help your Dad anymore. But it all works out, 'cause you got an expensive gift and you can't whine about that. I will take it away if you don't do all your chores."

# RANDOM GRAVEYARD MEMORIES

Being up early enough to catch the McDonald's breakfast menu. Eating McMuffins with newsprint like soot covering my fingers and hands, jeans stained black, shirt ruined. Like a chimney sweep or coal miner.

Going into Vons or Lucky's or a 7-Eleven with two dollars, alone, at two in the morning to get a Cherry Coke and a 3 Musketeers.

Watching my Dad throw newspapers up onto a four-story apartment balcony. Up that high and over a metal railing to land at someone's door. Not something I could do.

Trying to throw to a third-story balcony, hitting the picture window of an apartment hard with the thick Wednesday edition, watching the glass warble and bounce hoping it would break. Never did.

Gouging the top of my hand on the ashtray that jutted out from the dash of the Ford. Bleeding on newspapers as I folded.

> Watching my Dad hold a cigarette, drive, band a paper, and throw it all in one messy, busy, efficient motion. He smoked four to five packs a day. I have no memory of him without smoke.

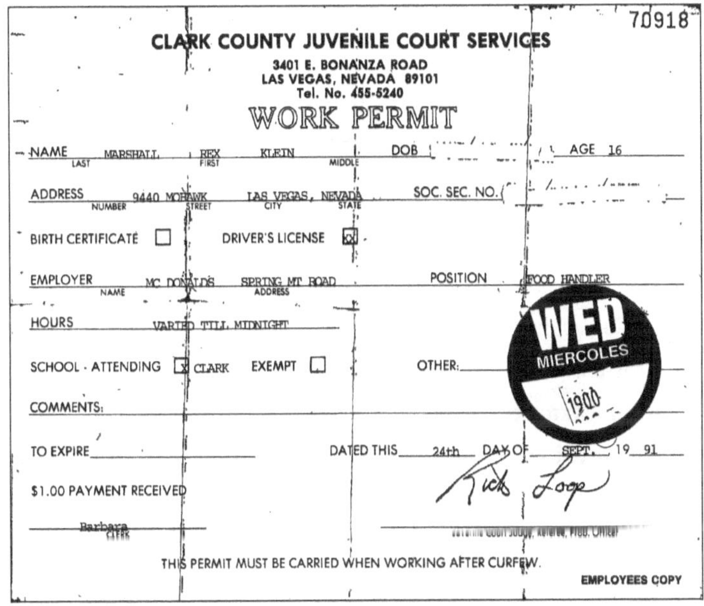

70918

CLARK COUNTY JUVENILE COURT SERVICES

3401 E. BONANZA ROAD
LAS VEGAS, NEVADA 89101
Tel. No. 455-5240

WORK PERMIT

NAME    MARSHALL    REX    KLEIN         DOB                    AGE  16
        LAST         FIRST   MIDDLE

ADDRESS    9440 MOHAWK    LAS VEGAS, NEVADA    SOC. SEC. NO.
           NUMBER   STREET   CITY      STATE

BIRTH CERTIFICATE ☐    DRIVER'S LICENSE ☒

EMPLOYER    MC DONALDS    SPRING MT ROAD    POSITION    FOOD HANDLER
        NAME            ADDRESS

HOURS        VARIED TILL MIDNIGHT

SCHOOL · ATTENDING ☒ CLARK  EXEMPT ☐    OTHER:

COMMENTS:

TO EXPIRE_______    DATED THIS___24th___DAY OF___SEPT.___19__91

$1.00 PAYMENT RECEIVED

Barbara
   CLERK

THIS PERMIT MUST BE CARRIED WHEN WORKING AFTER CURFEW.

EMPLOYEES COPY

# McDonald's

1991–92
$4.25–4.45/HOUR

We walked right in and got a job. Me and my only friend Benji. The interview was just a guy in a tucked-in awkward button-up asking me and my friend our names. The next day, I got a uniform and a stack of VHS tapes. I was told to sit in the break room and watch them all. I was left alone for two or three hours. I was ecstatic. I was hyper with happiness. I was getting four bucks an hour to watch movies. Really I only watched one and then just got bored and sat there, staring at the walls. I got eight bucks for doing nothing. I was feeling ambitious. Money was a new awesome world. I was excited. I was looking freedom in the face and aiming high.

I calculated my future. At (round it up because math is hard) four dollars an hour and forty a week, I could make 160 bucks a week. 640 a month. 7,680 a year. My mind was blown. I wanted to work more than forty a week. It wasn't fair. I saw my earnings maxed out. How could I ever make more money? I got my first check two weeks later. It was thirty dollars less than I figured. I had neglected to watch the video on taxes.

The assembly-line fast-food machine is really something. I still have scars from that job. And an intense dislike of any smells in my hair. They made it into a competition for us workers. How fast can you make twelve hamburgers? When you start they put you on Buns. Which means you just toast buns all day. You split twelve buns' tops and heels on these long trays which are put in a long, flat, griddle-type toaster. Slide them in, wait three or four minutes, slide them out. Watch that top handle of the toaster as you pull out. That's where the scars come from. Throw the tray to the condiment guy. Everything is laid out in quart-sized containers. Onions, pickles, tomatoes, sliced American. Four condiment guns: Mustard, Ketchup, Mayo, Big Mac Sauce. Shoot the tops with the guns. Pile the heels with the onions, pickles. Slap slap shoot shoot. Grill guy spatulas the hot meat pucks onto the dressed buns. Grill guy takes scars on the forearms from grease. Meat down, slap on the top of the bun. Lift the tray to the top shelf above the grill. The counter crew has the wrappers and they plop and quickly fold the burger up then drop it into a warmed holding tray. "We need twelve Macs and eight Quarters now!" would be the call. Or: "Drop three twelve-piece nuggets and one fish!" There was a separate fryer in the back part of the grill for nuggets and the infamous Fishwich.

The truck would come in about once a week. Everything in a McDonald's comes in frozen. Truck days were particularly brutal. We would hook up the roll-y ramp thing and chuck boxes of frozen meat down into the basement freezer. Backbreaking twisting and stacking in the freezer for hours. Crate of Quarter Pounder frozen pucks, fifty pounds. Crate of frozen Big Mac meat pucks, forty pounds. "You know what?" one of the old timers I was doing truck with professored. "The ingredients say 'other meat products ten percent.' You know what that means, man? It's eyeballs, man! They blend the cow eyes in the patties and that makes them freeze better. No joke! So many eyeballs, right??" I was uneasy about eating McDonald's after that revelation. But it was free, so I swallowed it down. Most people I know who worked fast food have a hard time eating it after being behind the curtain.

Derek was a short guy, very small frame but wide shoulders. Walked like he had an army behind him. Pure rooster confidence. He had longish hair and was very good at looking cool as he pulled it back with a hair tie while smoking and saying something nasty. He was the trouble I was too shy to become. I once drove him up and down the Strip while he French kissed in my backseat with his flirty blonde cousin. I watched in the rearview as they fondled and smacked mouths. I had never seen action so close. I saw their tongues touch. His hands went under her shirt. It was incredible and made me sad.

I was working the grill alone on a slow day when Derek busted into the kitchen.

"I just took an order at the window. This guy fucked over my Dad once. He doesn't remember me but I sure remember him. I'm making this one, Marshall. Stay out of my way and don't say shit."

I think the slip said "BIG MAC combo, no pick, + must." Derek grabbed the frozen patties and threw them on the grill. He salted them as was standard, flipped them when they bubbled brown. He then took the spatula and pushed the sizzling pucks into the grease trap on the side of the grill. The grease trap was a gutter on the far edge of the grill. Every time we scraped and cleaned the grill, we would push the water and boiling beef fat into the trap. At the end of the night, the closer had to pull out these four-foot-long traps and empty them. The smell was hard to explain and hard to stomach.

"You watch if anyone's coming," Derek said. His headset suddenly beeped and I could hear loud static through his ear piece. "Shit, I got another car." He grabbed a pair of tongs, pulled the two patties out of the trap and threw them back on the grill. "You let these fry and prep the bun and don't do anything before I get back." I toasted the three-piece bun, squeezed the condiment guns, threw on the diced onions and pickles. That smell never washed out of my fingers. Onions and pickles. I was brining in fast-food liquids. My hair was spray-coated in grease. My face had multiple erupting volcanoes.

Derek came running back to the grill. He pressed the patties with the spatula, lifted them and put them on the open bun. He looked me in the eye, his rebel ponytail thrust out of the back of his uniform hat, and cleared his throat. He leaned over the sandwich and carefully dropped a wad of spit into the bed of lettuce I had laid. He placed a pickle on top and swirled it around a bit to blend. He stacked the three sections perfectly, a trained professional, and placed the sandwich in the Big Mac box and took it up front.

"Order thirty-one is up, Rex was taking his time back there...." Derek said to the manager in front. The Mac was put in the bag with the rest of the order and handed out the drive-thru window. I felt numb about it. I bet the guy would have noticed a funky taste but still wolfed it down.

Cesar was a tall, suave Peruvian with shoulder-length black hair. He was a rock 'n' roller. His accent was thick, his English full of insults and cusses. He was twenty-two, which was godlike as I was sixteen. He gave me shit constantly. He called me Goofy in addition to a bunch of Spanish slang words that either meant "slow" or "retard," and loved to call me virgin. I never said I was but he would say, "Come on virgin, don't cry. I'll buy you a *Playboy* so you can jack off but don't let your mommy catch you, okay?" I would go to his apartment, he would drink and get stoned, and I would sit and watch and listen. He'd play Pink Floyd, Santana, Bread. I don't remember having much to say but he got a kick out of me. I could make him laugh. We played a lot of pool at a popular poolhouse. I had a car so that helped our friendship a lot.

"You don't drink. You don't smoke. You don't fuck. You like Adam Ant? You're turning Japanese, bro!"

We worked the grill together a lot, hustling burgers, stealing food, making fun of each other and everyone. We talked about music, he talked about girls. We talked major shit about our managers and jobs. He was a solid friend.

Then Cesar didn't show up for a couple weeks and he only occasionally had a working phone number so was always hard to reach. He was gone and no one was talking about it. I closed one night with the manager, a guy who had actually gone to McDonald's University but was still an okay person. Yes, there is or at least was a McDonald's University.

"Hey Alan, what happened to Cesar? Did he quit?"

"Ah, not exactly. He got deported. I don't know the details, really. I don't even know if his name was Cesar. Anyway, yeah, he was a mystery man." I vaguely understood he was illegal. It was so abrupt. Such a mystery. Work wasn't the same.

I got a call at my parents' house one night. "Hey virgin, stop jacking off, come and pick me up, man." It had been weeks. I picked Cesar up and we went to the one and only Arizona Charlie's. They had a forty-nine-cent breakfast. Two eggs, sausage, hashbrowns, toast for forty-nine cents. Forty-nine fucking cents. I once ordered two breakfasts. It was like being rich.

"Yeah, fuckin' shit, man. Police are fucking racists, man, you don't know. I was walking to work, you know, 'cause I don't have a fuckin' car 'cause I'm broke! Anyway, it's hot, I mean really hot, you know, and I'm walking with my bag an going to fucking McDonald's after I worked all night at the bar an shit. I had two fuckin' jobs, man! What the fuck. Anyway, I hear the fucking 'whoop whoop' of a police and then he's on the microphone like, 'Hey, stop walking, sir. Stop.' And I turn around and I'm like, 'What's up, man?' And the fuckin' cop is like, 'What are you doing out here?' Shit! Can you believe that shit? 'I'm walking to work, man.' And he goes, 'What's in the bag, sir?' Sir? Haha, shit, at least he called me sir. And I'm like, 'Hey, man, I work at McDonald's, man, I make hamburgers, man, I'm walking to work.' And he fuckin' says, 'I need to see your ID.' For what, man? For what? For hamburgers?

"Anyway, I don't have my ID, 'cause what the fuck? I'm going to McDonald's making fucking Big Macs! So I tell him I don't have it with me and he's like, 'What's in the bag?' And I'm like, 'My fucking uniform, man! It smells like onions, you wanna smell?' I mean, I didn't say that shit, come on. But man, he tells me to put the bag on the hood and my hands on the roof and he fucking checks me an grabs my nuts n shit and I'm like, hey, man! I don't like you like that! You gotta buy me a drink at least.

"And he puts me in the back and I'm like, shit, man, I'm gunna lose my McDonald's job but what the fuck, that job fuckin' sucks anyway. They take me to jail—'cause I was walking to work. Fuckin' pigs, man. And I gotta give them a different name 'cause I got arrested in L.A. and I got warrants on that name. That's how we gotta do it. They don't know. They think we're all Mexicans anyway. Then the INS gets in and they say, *Deported!*, and I'm like, shit, don't send me to Tijuana, man, I'm not a Mexican! Send me to Lima so I can see my familia.

"They put us on the bus and dropped us in TJ and I find a phone and call my friend in L.A. and I'm like, man, pick me up, man, I got deported. And he said, *Again?!* And I said, Oh shit, hook me up! And he got me a guy, this fuckin' kid he was like ten, and he walked for a little and he showed me this hole in the chain fence and we just walked through and I waited for hours in San Diego and had no money. My friend drove down and got me. I'm back! What's my name gunna be this time? Marshall? Rex Marshall? Ha, shit, I don't want a white virgin's name. I think my new name is Vegas. I keep coming back. Vegas sounds cool."

# RANDOM MCD'S MEMORIES

- Old gross guy named Carl, worked mornings usually. Disgusting, mostly toothless, greasy, large guy. Had a long and decrepit seventies car. Seats covered in dirty laundry and fast-food wrappers. He parked and always left Jesus radio on and the windows rolled down. "Well, if someone is gunna steal the car, I want them to hear the Good Book!" Whenever he got paid, he would say, "Ah, now I have enough to get some pretty lady to give me a pole-washing!"

- Benji and I had an informal competition of who could make the biggest burrito. They had tortillas as part of the "healthy" menu. I made one that was made of twenty-five McNuggets a handful of fries, ketchup, mustard, and lettuce. Took four tortillas. I snuck it into the break room and after eating the whole thing could barely stand up.

- I worked closing shifts a lot. Get out of school at three, work four to eleven. I took home whatever food didn't get sold. I would feed my little sister and myself with this for days. I felt victorious coming home with bags packed with salads, hamburgers, McNuggets, Big Macs. I was a good scrounge and still am.

"PEOPLE ARE OUR MOST IMPORTANT INGREDIENT"

## McDonald's Crew Performance Review

Rex Marshall
CREW PERSON'S NAME

**YOUR PERFORMANCE COUNTS…at McDONALD'S,** your performance is the key ingredient in our "pay for performance" philosophy. Performance reviews provide you and your manager the opportunity to discuss your performance, determine where you stand, and most importantly, how you can achieve greater success in the future. The performance review process enables us to clearly recognize individual contributions and see that employees receive fair compensation.

We encourage you to provide feedback on all or any of the areas of performance listed below:

03/19/92   4.25

DATE OF REVIEW:

What stations have S.O.C.'s been completed and communicated to the employee for this review period?

| | EXCEEDS STANDARDS | MEETS STANDARDS | DOES NOT MEET STANDARDS |
|---|---|---|---|
| **JOB PERFORMANCE** | | | |
| 1. Follows procedures in preparing all products according to McDonald's standards (SOC's) | | | ✓ |
| 2. Maintains speed and quality of counter and/or drive-thru service according to McDonald's standards (SOC's)  N/A | | | |
| 3. Maintains Q.S.C. standards, and enforces holding times | | | ✓ |
| 4. Hustles during rushes and helps out others when needed *talking / stands around* | | | ✓ |
| 5. Follows the practice of clean-as-you-go *grill area always mess* | | | ✓ |
| 6. Shows interest in self-development | | | ✓ |
| **ATTITUDE** | | | |
| 1. Works as a team member *doesn't help anyone else in grill* | | | ✓ |
| 2. Follows Management directions and observes store policies | | | ✓ |
| 3. Is friendly and courteous to customers and fellow employees | ✓ | | |
| **McDONALD'S IMAGE (Appearance)** | | | |
| 1. Wears a complete, neat, and clean uniform | | ✓ | |
| 2. Displays good personal hygiene | | ✓ | |
| **DEPENDABILITY** | | | |
| 1. Shows up as scheduled | | ✓ | |
| 2. Stays busy without direct supervision *no initiative* | | | ✓ |
| 3. Helps out in emergencies | | | ✓ |

**OVERALL RATING (Check One):**

☐ **OUTSTANDING** — Performance is always of exceptional quality; our best performers.  ☐ **EXCELLENT** — Performance consistently exceeds job requirements and expectations; significant contributor.  ☑ **GOOD** — Performance meets job requirements and expectations, steady contributor, job done well.  ☐ **NEEDS IMPROVEMENT** — Performance falls short of meeting job requirements and expectations.  ☐ **UNSATISFACTORY** — Performance is unacceptable; has significantly failed to meet job requirements.

**COMMENTS:**

MAJOR ACHIEVEMENTS:

MAJOR PERFORMANCE AREAS NEEDING IMPROVEMENT:

CREW FEEDBACK:

PAY INCREASE AMOUNT: 10¢ /4.35   EFFECTIVE DATE OF INCREASE: 03/   DATE OF NEXT PAY REVIEW: 09/19/92

Rex Marshall   /   /   03/19/92
CREW'S SIGNATURE   DATE   MANAGER'S SIGNATURE   DATE

**McDonald's**

*My first performance review on 3/19/92. Note that in nine of the thirteen categories (I was N/A for the Drive-Thru category as I refused to train there) I was marked DOES NOT MEET STANDARDS. The notes, written in a fine 90s cursive, are quite rich. Two of three categories marked bad in ATTITUDE. I remember getting grilled (pun intended) about how bad an employee I was. I still was given a ten-cent raise.*

"PEOPLE ARE OUR MOST IMPORTANT INGREDIENT"

## McDonald's Crew Performance Review

#31   REX MARSHALL
CREW PERSON'S NAME

YOUR PERFORMANCE COUNTS…at McDONALD'S, your performance is the key ingredient in our "pay for performance" philosophy. Performance reviews provide you and your manager the opportunity to discuss your performance, determine where you stand, and most importantly, how you can achieve greater success in the future. The performance review process enables us to clearly recognize individual contributions and see that employees receive fair compensation.

We encourage you to provide feedback on all or any of the areas of performance listed below.

9/23/92
DATE OF REVIEW:

What stations have S.O.C.'s been completed and communicated to the employee for this review period?

| | EXCEEDS STANDARDS | MEETS STANDARDS | DOES NOT MEET STANDARDS |
|---|---|---|---|
| **JOB PERFORMANCE** | | | |
| 1. Follows procedures in preparing all products according to McDonald's standards (SOC's)   10:1 DOES | | | X |
| 2. Maintains speed and quality of counter and/or drive-thru service according to McDonald's standards (SOC's)   N/A | | | |
| 3. Maintains O.S.C. standards, and enforces holding times | | X | |
| 4. Hustles during rushes and helps out others when needed | | X | |
| 5. Follows the practice of clean-as-you-go | | X | |
| 6. Shows interest in self-development | | | X |
| **ATTITUDE** | | | |
| 1. Works as a team member | | X | |
| 2. Follows Management directions and observes store policies | | X | |
| 3. Is friendly and courteous to customers and fellow employees | | | |
| **McDONALD'S IMAGE** (Appearance) | | | |
| 1. Wears a complete, neat, and clean uniform | | | X |
| 2. Displays good personal hygiene | | | X |
| **DEPENDABILITY** | | | |
| 1. Shows up as scheduled | | X | |
| 2. Stays busy without direct supervision | | | X |
| 3. Helps out in emergencies | | | X |

**OVERALL RATING** (Check One):

☐ OUTSTANDING
—Performance is always of exceptional quality; our best performers.

☐ EXCELLENT
—Performance consistently exceeds job requirements and expectations; significant contributor

☒ GOOD
—Performance meets job requirements and expectations; steady contributor, job done well.

☐ NEEDS IMPROVEMENT
—Performance falls short of meeting job requirements and expectations.

☐ UNSATISFACTORY
—Performance is unacceptable; has significantly failed to meet job requirements.

**COMMENTS:**

MAJOR ACHIEVEMENTS:   LEARNED ALL STATIONS IN GRILL

MAJOR PERFORMANCE AREAS NEEDING IMPROVEMENT:   NEED TO "BRANCH OUT" LEARN WINDOW.

CREW FEEDBACK:

PAY INCREASE AMOUNT: .10¢     EFFECTIVE DATE OF INCREASE: 9/23/92     DATE OF NEXT PAY REVIEW: 3/23/93

SIGNATURE     DATE 9/23/92     MANAGER'S SIGNATURE     DATE 9/23/92

ORIGINAL COPY - EMPLOYEE

*On my next performance review, six months later on 9/23/92, I had drastically improved. Like a new worker risen from the ashes of shame. I met standards in nine of the thirteen categories. Four of my Xs were placed in the gray area between MEETS and DOES NOT. Which is a still a win and shows how hard I tried in those six months to be a better cog in the Mikey D's burger machine.*

*Again, I was awarded a ten-cent raise.*

# Michaels Arts and Crafts

1992–94
$4.50/HOUR

I was trained consistently and ruthlessly for maybe two weeks. Shown how to stock the paint aisle. How to hang the fake flowers. How to set up an entire display using a detailed blueprint. Endcaps and selling techniques. How to run the cash register, which I was bad at. I was too nervous and could never count change. Just like McD's, I wanted to stay behind the scenes. I learned all about wicker baskets. I studied plastic flowers and a variety of glues. I memorized what kind of paint was good for sweatshirts. How to use this thing called a Bedazzler. Choosing paint brushes and calligraphy nibs. Taking things out to people's cars. I volunteered to pick up trash in the parking lot all the damn time.

After my probation, I noticed things were pretty lax. I was on my own. I stocked things, had my section. I took over paints and brushes, which I soon found was a pain. But I could pick and choose what to work on. I found out quickly I could pick Not Working, which looked just like work! Holding a clipboard was a great technique. Just holding it, maybe furrowing the eyebrows a bit and walking away with a frustrated stride. Carrying a broom was fantastic. Holding an empty cardboard box was okay. Stealing was maybe the best method. If you could steal right, you could make it seem like you were working. You have never looked so busy as that time you were trying to not get caught stealing. I didn't break bad right away. It took some getting fucked with to turn me.

We had a framing department. The store made major cash over there. Always busy. Just a few guys were trained for that job. They had a ton of orders but always, without fail, found time to fuck off. They would stockpile glass that needed to be trashed. Cut-offs or accidentally chipped pieces or whatever. They would pile it up for weeks. Then would come Smash Day. We took turns at the trash compactor, throwing all that waiting glass against the back metal wall of the dumpster. The noise was pure joy. Best day of the month. Stock people like me would save all kinds of stuff for Smash Day. Half-sheets of glass, broken vases, flower pots. Those goddamn wicker baskets. If I was tired of stocking a product I would sometimes throw it in the dumpster and do that clapping-hands-like-you-are-slapping-the-dust-off gesture. All done! I got all that product taken care of. What a day, I'm taking my fifteen!

The store manager was a round guy named Albert. He wore a suit and tie and you could tell he hated it. You could see in the way his shirt pinched his neck that he wanted to wear a shitty T-shirt and flip-flops. He must have jumped into his sweats as soon as he got home. Somehow the crew got organized and we went out for food after closing.

Albert had just moved out from the Midwest, had an unclear marriage and was alone in Vegas. One of the framing guys thought

Bossman was lonely and invited him out with us. I was seventeen and worried about being kicked out of the bar. We saw Albert through the window as he pulled up in his sad sedan. I felt that everyone was feeling sorry for this guy. Rumors of him working overtime, renting a cheap apartment, and not having friends.

He found our table in the corner and sat down, shook hands with us. He was trying not to be a boss, but he was the boss. It was not comfortable. Thom was the brave one, he asked the tough questions. "So Albert, why are you in this shithole? Michaels in Vegas? They don't have them in Indiana?"

"Haha, yes. Well, I was offered this job and I thought it would be a good chance to scout out living in Vegas," chuckled Albert.

"You're all alone out here? What about your wife?" Thom probed.

"Well, yes, I have a son and my wife. They are both in Michigan, it wasn't practical to get them out here yet. But you know, soon, once I get my footing here, you know, haha. I'll get them out here in a few months," said the boss.

I could tell that none of my coworkers believed him. We ordered nachos, tots, beers, chicken wings. A bar food buffet. I ate everything but didn't drink. Albert ordered a fair share, had enough beer to make himself silly. The conversation was mostly work-related, standard complaining. A couple of the guys got into it about sports. Another night of forgettable bar talk.

The check came and it wasn't huge, but it wasn't small either. There are some people who love this part of the night, the mathematics of the split check. We all laid down our cash until it came to Albert. He pulled out his wallet and made a whimpering sound.

"Hey guys, aw jeez, this is pretty embarrassing. But, well, I don't seem to have any cash, haha. Um, I'm really sorry, I worked late and haven't gone out in awhile and didn't go to the bank." He put his hands up in the air as he talked, like he was surrendering to forces outside of his control.

"Ah, the boss doesn't have money!" said Thom.

"God, I know! It's awful, I'm so embarrassed!" cried Albert.

"Aw, it's cool, Albert. Who can throw in for the boss tonight?"

I checked my wallet and I had an extra twenty. Thom saw and snatched it. "Ah ha! Stock boy has cash! Good job, Rex! You've saved the boss!" Thom hollered with glee.

"Aw, Rex, thanks so much. I'll get you back tomorrow, you work tomorrow? I'll get you back, thanks again, I'm so sorry," Albert groveled.

The next day at work I saw Albert briefly as he walked from his office to the bathroom. "Hey, Albert! How's it going?" I asked. "Oh hey, Rex, good good," said my supervisor. I didn't see him the next day, or much the next week. He was in his office, I saw him back there as I clocked in and out.

Maybe a week after I had paid for Albert's food, Mike, the Assistant Manager, found me in the basket aisle. "Hey Rex, Albert wants to see you in his office. Drop what you're doing for a minute, you can come back to it."

I stepped into the office. "Oh hey, Albert, how's it going, man?" I thought he could have just handed me the money on the floor. Maybe this was more professional.

"Go ahead and close the door and sit down," said the boss. "So, look, I'll just come right out and get to the point. You are always late to your shifts, and your lunch breaks are always long. I look at all the timecards, Rex. You need to get here on time and be ready to work when you clock in. Being five minutes late may not seem like a big deal to you, but I have a whole store to run. I have to write you up for this. Sign on the line there that you understand. This is strike one. Don't get to three strikes, you know what happens then," said the boss.

I had to sign to verify that I had read and understood this disciplinary notice. I went back out to the floor. I went outside and hid in my car for a while. I stole a bunch of paint. I threw a Bedazzler in the trash. He never brought up paying me back and I never had the nerve to bring it up.

# RANDOM CRAFT MEMORIES

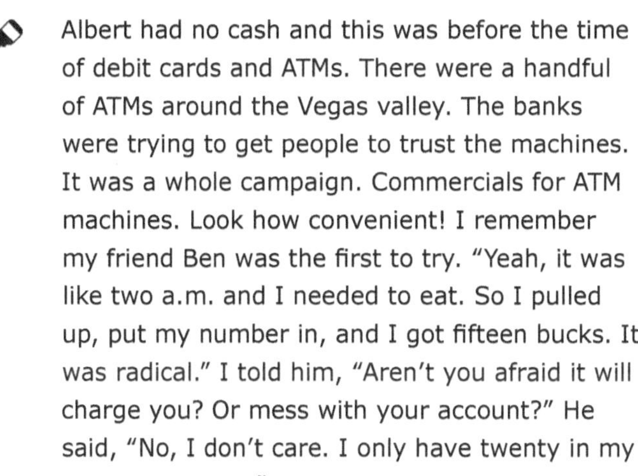

Albert had no cash and this was before the time of debit cards and ATMs. There were a handful of ATMs around the Vegas valley. The banks were trying to get people to trust the machines. It was a whole campaign. Commercials for ATM machines. Look how convenient! I remember my friend Ben was the first to try. "Yeah, it was like two a.m. and I needed to eat. So I pulled up, put my number in, and I got fifteen bucks. It was radical." I told him, "Aren't you afraid it will charge you? Or mess with your account?" He said, "No, I don't care. I only have twenty in my account anyway."

I stole so much shit from this job it was incredible. I traded paints for car stereo gear. I tried to paint and was pissed at myself for how awful I was.

I recently found a T-shirt that said "I'M QUITTING MICHAELS....AGAIN" in iron-on letters. Everyone I worked with signed it. I have little memory of these people. I do not remember quitting and coming back. Maybe I did after my Eugene excursion. I do remember I got my friend Benji my job when I left. Yes, Benji from McD's. He just stopped going to McD's after like a month. He didn't really need that job like I did. He did need my Michaels job, though, and I handed it to his lazy ass.

# McDonald's Eugene, OR

1993

$4.75/HOUR

After I graduated high school, I tried to take myself to college. For reasons I forget, I heard that Eugene, Oregon was the place to be. Cesar, my buddy from Vegas, my deported friend from McDonald's, came with me. He'd been working at a casino and living in a beat-up apartment under the eyesore of the Vegas World casino and the half-completed, recently-half-on-fire Stratosphere tower. He'd been hanging with Camacho, a coke dealer who was pressuring Cesar to get in the game. So much money but so much risk. I said, "Hey, I'm moving to Oregon tomorrow night." He said, "Yeah? Shit. Okay, fuck it. Pick me up tomorrow, nine p.m." I got to his apartment, he threw one gym bag in the back of my Chevy Cavalier wagon and said, "Yeah, let's go. Vegas is shit."

We stumbled around Eugene for a week, slept in the wagon, got woken up by cops. There were no places to live and no places to work. College was back in session and all the places were full. I had never known this was a possibility—that a city could have no vacant apartments. I had never been to that small of a town before. A college town, no less. A place where the stores and restaurants closed at night. I was a twenty-four-hour guy from a sprawling metropolis. Growing up in Las Vegas makes you a stranger to normal society. We finally found a weekly motel where we slept, covered in mice and fleas.

Our situation got desperate and there it was, calling to us like a neglected mother. We couldn't ignore it because it was on the main road, those goddamn skyscraping glowing arches. We laughed about it at first, the thought of going to work at another McDonald's. About a week later, we were broke enough to overcome our shame. The manager welcomed us with open arms. She was over the moon to hire a couple of grill veterans. She asked why we left Vegas. I can't remember what we said. Cesar and I laughed for weeks at how dumb and pitiful we were.

It was a surreal defeat to be working at another McDonald's. I was a thousand miles from my home McDonald's but I knew where everything was. I was faster than my trainer at the grill. I could make a run of twelve hamburgers while he made one McChicken. I was from a massive city, the big city McDonald's. I was a high-volume, high-pressure, fast-food machine. I felt myself become proud when I felt fast at something for the first time. Then I looked in the break room mirror. I had that hat on again. I smelled like onion and pickle brine again. My war against pimples: not going well. They were back on the battlefield taking back all the land I had won back.

The manager there, damn I wish I could remember her name. She called me the "walking Quaalude." I asked her what that was, she said, "You know, mellow... like you're stoned all the time.

'Cause you are, right? It's cool! That's why you moved to Eugene, right?" I didn't want to get into it and explain that I hated drugs. I guess I was abnormally chill. I don't know.

Cesar, however, went out and got stoned with her once. He went to a bar with the closing shift team. "Shit, man, I thought she was a lesbian, man! But we had a joint and then she was lookin' at me like that, oh man, I had to get outta there. Fuck! She might kick my ass now that I didn't fuck her."

It snowed that winter. I had only seen snow once in my life (it snowed in Vegas twice in the seventies!) but I was a toddler and only remembered the vague sense of cold and white. Cesar had never seen it in his life, coming from Peru. He was thrilled at first. Then the cold got to him. He put on all his clothes and was shivering. We bought blankets at Kmart and they were no better than wrapping ourselves in toilet paper. The wall heaters barely whispered. There were fleas jumping off our legs, exploding from the cruddy carpet as you walked across. Mice crawled in the walls and ate any food we left in the cupboards or on the counter. I had completed one class at the University of Oregon and spent all the savings my Gramma had given me. I got a C in Archeology and my Indiana Jones fantasy was hitting the fan. We said, fuck it, let's get back to Vegas. The dynamic duo left the Eugene McDonald's. I never worked fast food or any kind of food thing ever again.

I had gotten two or three speeding tickets in Eugene. I couldn't fathom how people could drive so slow. One cop who pulled me over saw my Nevada plates and had his hand on his gun as he asked me why I was "street racing." By the time I got back to

Vegas, I learned my license was suspended. On top of that, a couple weeks later my Mom kicked me out of the house. I hid in my girl-friend's closet for months. Her parents must have known. I found a temp agency and had a whole list of mind-numbing and/or body-crushing work. I went mostly for the mind-numbing. Maybe body-breaking is better? I grabbed every job I could to claw and slither my way out of the neon-nuked bowl of Las Vegas. Eugene wasn't the place, and I could see the writing on the wall for Vegas. I was homeless and needed cash. I found a temp agency and soon enough the phone started ringing.

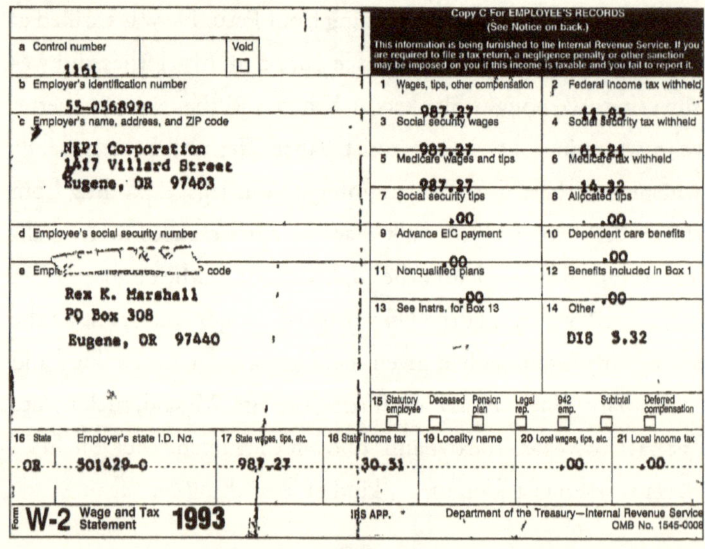

# TEMP JOBS: VEGAS

## GRATEFUL DEAD CONCERT

SILVER BOWL, LAS VEGAS, NV
6/26/94
$4.25/HOUR

Maybe my most utterly confusing temp job. Temp jobs were often sloppy, but this one was a true shitshow. The agency told me to show up at the Silver Bowl, the biggest arena in Vegas at the time. I got there and found the employee zone. They gave me a polo shirt, a walkie-talkie, and a bottle of water. Then they sent me to the chain-link perimeter set up around the entrance of the stadium. I walked way out there. They had a temp standing out there about every 200 yards. Each person had a section of fence they had to keep an eye on.

The job was simple enough. Make sure people didn't try to sneak in. The fence was about fifteen feet high, and set up as a perimeter around the massive covered stadium dome. It was hot out. Not summer-hot, but not "let's climb the hot metal fifteen-foot-high fence" hot either. The backstory to this job (which they explained in about three sentences) was that in a couple of towns, the Deadheads had grouped up and attacked a portion of the fence and made it collapse. Instead of one or two hippies going up and over, they sent dozens over until the fence crumpled and fell. At one of the shows, a few people had gotten seriously hurt. Event organizers were panicking. They hired temps to stop the potential siege of the Silver Bowl.

The longer I stood out there with my bottle of water in the sun, the more I realized how utterly powerless I was to stop any horde from crashing the castle fence. They had told me to yell STOP or tell the siegers I could walkie the police. I was still a shy kid. I could yell loud, sure, but I was not skilled in yelling at people. What could I actually do to stop an antpile of hippies from climbing on each other's tye-dyed backs and toppling the chain link? Not to mention it was incredibly, brain damaging-ly boring out there. Just standing there. Being a "deterrent." I weighed about 120 pounds. A couple kids came up to the fence. "Hey, man, we could totally push this down, right?" "I dunno," I said. "I mean, I guess?" They looked up the height of the fence and walked off.

I had made up my mind that if a mass of hippies congealed at my section of the fence I wasn't going to do shit. I was not going to get smashed underneath like a security martyr. It never came to that anyway. After a few hours of pacing in circles and staring at the asphalt, I realized I had not seen a single person in hours. I looked from side to side and saw that, in fact, I was the last temp still standing out there. I felt like an idiot and decided my work was done. I strolled back to the meeting place where I had entered and found it abandoned. I was lost on what to do with myself. So, I walked all the way back to the stadium, went up a ramp, and sauntered into a maelstrom of hippie chaos.

Immediately I stumbled into a mass of swirling barefoot danc-
ers. The floors were soaking wet. I remember almost slipping. It
was extremely humid in there. Wet sauna feeling. The place was
huge. 20 or 30k full to the brim. So many twirling dreads. Men
and women topless and writhing. I watched the Dead. They were
little dots from where I was standing. Jerry was down there. I still
don't care for their music, but am happy to brag that I saw them.
Their jammy wall of sound bounced and slurped off the sweaty
throngs. There were dance trains of people, some of them twenty
long at least, running like snakes through the aisles. It was alive in
there. It was something. There was no security in sight. They must
have abandoned post like I did.

## PLASTIC CUP FACTORY

### JEAN, NV
### 1994
### $4.25/HOUR

Jean, Nevada is a place that shouldn't have a name. They could just
call it Exit 12 and be done. There are a handful of things in Jean.
There are two casinos, the Gold Spike and Nevada Landing. There
is a state prison. There is a gas station. There is a micro airport.
There are no residents of Jean, Nevada. There are no houses and
yes, no one lives there. It's a pit stop. Workers drive down there to
work either from Vegas or the border town of Primm. It is thirty
minutes south of Las Vegas in the thick of the Mojave, right on
Interstate 15. Oh, and there is a plastic factory where I probably
took a hit on my life expectancy by working there for two months.

The machines were the size of trains. They spit out plastic cups and yogurt quarts twelve hours a day. The warehouse-sized factory was shellacked with an invisible fog of burnt plastic fumes. I was forced to work a large cup machine. Five quarts. The cups popped out at the top, fell down a metal slide and onto a table where I had to snatch them. They had to be stacked by the dozen, dropped in a large cardboard box. You had to make the box, catch the cups, make sure they were not oily or warped, stack them, throw them in a box, and then seal the box and stack the boxes neatly on a pallet. Enthralling, monotonous work.

The woman training me was missing two fingers. She had worked at the plastic plant for nearly twenty years. She was rail-thin and pointed at things with her cigarette. "They get stuck up here, and you can use your broom to knock them back, or maybe get your hand in there real quick. Watch out right here and here, though, those are bad spots. If you got a jam there, hit this big red button and it rings the alarm bell. If you don't keep up, these cups will melt and you could catch the thing on fire. I'll show you what the rhythm is, here. Watch."

She turned it on, made a box with the tape gun, put a plastic bag liner in the new box. The cups started falling, a waterfall of empty yogurt buckets. The fumes of hot plastic. The cups jumped like popcorn. She stacked them by the dozen, pivoted on her feet to the box behind her, filled it with ten rows of cups, and then sealed the box and put it on the pallet. Then she made another box, put in the plastic liner, and the cups were backed up on the slide. Probably forty of the cups had fallen in less than five minutes. She was a veteran pro. In control. She grabbed a stack, and another, and repeated the process of filing, sealing, stacking, and making another box.

She waved me to get closer. Her waving hand was the hand missing two fingers.

"Alright, I got you a head start here... your box is made and taped and this machine is warmed up. I'm gunna hand it to you, now, you just keep it moving, don't let it back up! Oh, and if they come out all greasy or with oil, ring this bell and a mechanic will run over. Okay, here ya go, your first box, it's all yours." She patted me on the shoulder. The cups were coming to meet me.

I kept up longer than I thought I would before I had to slam that red button. It was so goddamn fast. The amount of tasks I had to do was insane. The tape gun ran out of tape. My box fell off the pallet. I misgrabbed a stack of cups and they went in the box sideways and fucked up the rows. That damn machine kept shooting the cups and eventually they were so jammed that I couldn't even pull them out. I slammed the big red button of failure.

A very loud bell, like an air raid alarm clock, went off. Two mechanics in greasy baseball caps came running over. "What the hell is going on!" one of them shouted at me as he ran and jumped on the side of the machine. He climbed the machine like a familiar cliff. He got to the top, tried to reach in and grab the cup that was stuck and melting in there. He punched out a whole wad of brown and half-melted cups. The machine was still fucking pumping them out.

Another mechanic put in a key and the machine shuddered and died. The lady who had trained me came running over. I forget her name, but the mechanic said it very angrily and called her to him. He threw a couple of my melted cups on the floor. He pointed at them, at me, then point-blank madly pointed at her. She was apologetic. Submissive and talking fast. She took over the machine while I made the boxes and pushed a broom. At lunch I gummed a weak sandwich and felt my head pulse from the fumes.

Driving out there five days a week was maddening. In other circumstances, I deeply love Nevada and the lonely asphalt of those desert highways. I've driven up, down, across, and through most of that magical wasteland. (Of course I've seen UFOs, duh.) Driving forty minutes to nowhere to work a job that is probably poisoning your body and brain and taking you nowhere was a bit much. It is basically the Autobahn out there, but still, I couldn't drive fast enough back home. I tried not to look at the clock while working but silently yelled at every minute. I held on out there, even though I couldn't ever get quick enough to take over a machine on my own, for about three weeks. The headaches were intense. I wanted to run away every day. I buckled down like only the desperate are able to do. I finally had three hundred dollars in my pocket. I packed and bought a Greyhound ticket.

That was the last job I had in Vegas.

# Temp Jobs: Portland, OR

## 1994
### $5/HOUR

Everything I salvaged from my young dumb life fit in a foot locker and a backpack. The Greyhound cost forty dollars, I think. Portland felt like an overgrown village, a valley with a gluttony of green. The city was dense with creative movement. People outdoors all the time. All the bushes and vines and gardens and massive skyscraping trees. I had only seen gardens a few times in my life. I had stepped out of cactus land into a spewing cornucopia.

I looked in the paper. White pages, yellow pages, *Nickel* ads. The *Nifty Nickel*. Mostly crossed things out with my pen. I found a temp employment place by my house, filled out a book's worth of paperwork. Lied about experience. Lied about how long I had lived in Portland. Lied about being able to do 10-Key. I can lift 900 pounds, so don't worry about seventy-five. Yes, I can work nights and weekends. Of course I know how to type (still don't). I ate Top Ramen, boiled potatoes, and obsessively looked for that blinking light on the answering machine.

## Shoe Store

Got placed at a shoe store out in Clackamas near the mall. They were doing an inventory, putting alarm tags on every upscale tennis shoe. The tag was this big, black, plastic anti-shoplifter tab that had to be pinned to the tongue of every left foot. It took a special tool, almost like pliers, to attach the thing. After around two hours, my hand was cramping. Lunch was maybe thirty minutes. I did not want to come back. I chatted with this tough-looking guy.

"Man, this doesn't end!" he said. "Look at all these shoes. But you know what? When we done, then they let us go. So, man, you got to slow it down. We get paid by hours and you got to stretch 'em. We got to stretch this job to last the week!" I slowed down as much as was humanly possible and found that to be more work than the actual job.

## Call Center

I have vague memories of working at a call center. Hopefully an extinct job. No, nevermind, I get spam calls daily. "Hello, do you have any property you want to sell?" etc. etc. forever and ever. This was a large office in a strip mall somewhere in SW Portland. No idea what the company name was. They sat me down at a small desk-cubicle-thing with about thirty others. I had a ream of paper on a clipboard next to my phone. This stack was a list of people's names and phone numbers. There were codes next to each name and the names were sorted by these codes.

A trainer sat with me my first day. He handed me my headset, which I clumsily put on my head and over my ear. I did not want to know what I looked like with that thing on. "Okay, so Rex, this is your list of clients. We want you to start with the ones here on the first page. These are people who have already bought or given money. After you get warmed up and grab a few of those, we want you to go over to the cold list. The cold list is people that may have mailed in something, but have never bought or phoned. You will be breaking the ice!" he said.

At my desk was the phone, the headset for the phone so I could be hands-free, the stack of names and numbers, and most importantly: my almighty script. All I had to do was dial the number, and if someone picked up: ask for the person on the list, then read the script. My first day I dialed up around twenty-five people and they all said no thanks or hung up before I could get the whole script read. The trainer came over. "Hey, so we were listening in on the last few calls you made, yeah, so you just hung up the phone after they said no. That's not how we do things. We are never the one to hang up first. Also, we do not *let* them hang up, do you understand? If you hear them hesitate or hem and haw, you go to the second page of the script where we have a different approach written out. The whole point of calling them is to get the sale. We do not take no for an answer. You want to close every call!"

On my long bus ride home after that first shift, I thought about what it would take for me to keep people on the phone. I would have to become a very different person. I would have to connive and manipulate and badger. I would have to demand a yes. Or at the very least annoy people into surrender. Long story short, I lasted all of two days with that dorky headset. When I called someone and they said NO THANKS or GO AWAY I did not have it in me to trick them or use some veiled psych-ops to get their credit card info. I simply said Okay and hung up the phone.

My trainer said I wasn't putting my heart into it and I said yes, you're right, I'm not doing that at all.

## Office Closet Somewhere in SW Portland

Again, another long bus trip to the suburbs. Beaverton, I think. An office worker, very outgoing and friendly, showed me into a closet. Boxes of receipts, stuffed file folders, and mile-long folded tapestries of dot matrix print jobs stacked front to back to front again, almost touching the ceiling.

"We need you to put these in order. Maybe by date? I don't think all of them have dates. You get it?"

"What do I do with the ones that don't have dates?"

"Just put them in order as best you can?"

"You mean, guess?"

"Well, I don't know what my supervisor wants and she isn't here today. So, I mean, don't guess, but read them and maybe that will give a clue. Okay? Take your time."

I spent five or six hours in that closet, looking at print-outs and spreadsheets that made no sense to me. The office had been stacking boxes of files in this closet for years. Not stacking in any order, more opening the door and chucking boxes and slamming the door.

At the end of the day, the girl came back.

"Did you finish?"

"Well, no. I got through maybe two stacks? Might take a couple more days."

"Oh. Well. Okay, you can take off for the day. Thanks!"

I got a phone call the next day that the office didn't want me to come in the next day. They said I was too slow.

# Selling Plasma

1994

$40 FOR FIRST TIME, $25 EACH TIME AFTER

I had a period of panic when the temp jobs dried up and the classifieds had nothing. I walked around Hawthorne with my typewritten resume and struck out for weeks. There were very few Help Wanted signs. I was twenty and had no safety net. I heard about selling blood. A friend of mine had tried it. There was an ad in the *Nickel* that said you could make $100 a month. My rent was $300. Desperation led me to selling my body and its fluids. Actual blood money was yelling my name.

After completing a thick clipboard of entry form questions, I was called into a tiny office. An overworked man went over a few points. Have you ever used needles for drugs? Do you have any tattoos? Are you a homosexual? Do you have any infectious disease like Hepatitis? Are you currently sick with a cold or flu?

The first time was fine. My blood came out as I zoned out with the TV. Free juice and cookies when you were done. Forty bucks in my pocket. Next visit, a new hire hooked me up. She wanted to tap my right arm but I had a probably illogical thought that it might ruin my favorite arm so I surrendered my left.

I didn't think much when it seemed like she was stumbling around on my arm. She tied me off, tapped here and there, pinched the little rope highway of liquid gold under my arm. She stuck me, made a disgruntled sound, pulled it out. Slapped my bicep hard. She jammed the needle in again, said this vein wasn't the best. But the tube filled with my red juice and we were good to go.

I let my head relax back against the headrest and I think *RoboCop* was on one of the TVs. One of the greatest movies of all time, but maybe not for right that moment. I watched the blood fill the tube into the centrifuge next to my chair. I then watched as the blood stopped flowing. It began as a stutter in the stream. Little squirts of blood came out instead of the nice flow. Okay, panic time. There was quickly nothing coming out of my vein anymore. The machine was still spinning and trying to pull blood out of me. It sure did look like my arm was sucked dry and was dead.

I put up my hand. The tech I already had misgivings about came over. Checked my dry tube. I tried my best not to lose my shit but my shit was spilling over the sides. "Okay, that's not good. What is going on?" I said with a little shake in my voice. I was very uneasy.

"Ah, I must have hit it wrong. Hold on." And what she did next made me get up and never sell plasma again.

The needle in my arm was probably an inch long. Not a sew-your-buttons-back-on-with-a-tiny-needle-and-thread kinda needle. This was a hollow steel nail. Thick and long and in my vein, in my blood, in my arm.

This tech woman said, "I'm new here. I must have not gone deep enough." And she got ahold of the needle and jammed it deeper into my vein. And at the same time, she LIFTED the needle so the skin of my arm pulled up like flour dough. It looked like she was sawing a log and the needle was the saw and my arm was the log. In and out and grab-push-pull-deep-jab-jam. My skin like Laffy Taffy. My eyes popped out of my head.

"Okay, this is hurting me," I said. "Just stop."

"Well, if I could get at that right arm. See? Lots of good ones there," she said in a certifiably creepy tone.

"No, I'm done. Pull that out. I'm done," I said with more fear than anger. Was my arm going to die? Did I just get my arm murdered for twenty-five bucks??

"Well, you won't get the full twenty-five if you leave now."

"I don't care, get me out of here. Get that out of me." Again, I wasn't mad. I was truly scared.

I was terrified of making a scene but I was miles past my comfort zone. Her supervisor came over and they shamed me. Others getting their blood sucked out lazily stared. The staff treated me like a quitter. The woman who messed up the tap. The annoyed supervisor. I got paid a sad twenty. The way the money handler put the cash in my hand was gross. I was a weak failure and they looked at me as a sad loser who couldn't go the distance. I had a large bruise on my arm for about two weeks and thought of the image of my skin being lifted off my arm with a giant needle for over a decade.

# PJ's Sleep Shop

1994 FOR ONE DAY
$50

The classifieds had no jobs and I had walked around looking for Help Wanted signs and had nothing to show for it. I was collecting cans for money. I didn't have the gas turned on that winter to save cash. I tied my comforter over my shoulders and sat in front of the oven. I had no parents or safety net. There was the very real thought of not finding enough money to live. I was twenty and not making it.

I was at a bus stop on Hawthorne and 20th when an old guy came at me, waving his arms. "Hey! Hey you! You need a job? You want to work?"

"I do, yeah, really?"

"Yeah, get here tomorrow, nine a.m. I got a job for you. Be here at nine. PJ's Sleep Shop."

I got there at nine and all the old dudes in there had no idea who I was but they were cool. One of them gave me some busy work. "Okay, sweep all this and just wait, alright? You'll be out for most of the day."

PJ, the namesake and boss of the place, introduced me to a guy who looked like an ex-con. He had a smaller pickup, a Nissan, I think. I opened the passenger door and a pit bull sat in the seat. "Just climb on in and push her over, she'll move." She had a head the size of a watermelon. Pit bulls have the deepest eyes of all the dogs. Gazing in, I saw she was a sweet baby. I gave her a pat and she lifted and then plopped her muzzle on my lap.

Mattresses are truly unruly. They do not obey physics. You go right and the mattress goes left. You measure a hallway to see if it will fit and it will never fit. Even if you use lasers to plot the course, the mattress will flop off and heave you towards the path of most resistance.

I grabbed one and got it up some stairs and it was tough, but I had first-timers luck. Back in the truck, the guy said, "Alright, you handled that like a pro, man! You just gotta grab those fuckers and tell 'em who's boss. Nice work."

"Man, this job can be strange," the maybe-ex-con said. "These things can break your back, that's for sure. I had one delivery and this fine woman opened the door. And I went in and looked at where she wanted the thing and I got out my tape and said, Okay, well, it isn't going to fit, ma'am. Not at all! And she was like, Oh no, really? And I was like, Oh no, really not! But, I'll tell you what. The mattress can fold up that hall staircase fine. The box spring, well, I can break it in half and squeeze it through, but you'll have to sign something that says you wanted me to do that. That's what we did, I broke the thing! Cracked it with my boots and folded it like a pancake and jammed it down that hall and it was fine once it was put on the frame and flat again.

"And then you know what? Man, this woman was a fox. She says, Well, do you want to help me make sure this bed works? And she unbuttons a couple on her top! She was hot, man! I could have fucked her on that new bed! But I told her I had to get back to work. She probably had a husband. It was crazy. It was just too much!"

Back at PJ's I swept up the place and the guy I rode with put in a good word for me. PJ handed me fifty. "Thanks for the help today. You really saved us. I heard you were good out there, but this was a one-time deal 'cause I had a guy call in sick. Thanks again."

# GOODWILL

1995–96
$5/HOUR

The old Goodwill on 7th looked like an old mill building from the 1800s. I believe it actually was a mill. A leaning three-story yellow shack dusted in asbestos and the powdered bones of working men. I interviewed there and thought I would work in the best thrift store I had ever seen, but that was not to be. I was sent to a warehouse out near Milwaukie to sort and price new donations for the new store. The ancient yellow shithouse was being torn down. They were building a brand-spanking-new place in the parking lot. The old building was destined to be the new parking lot.

I could walk to the old Goodwill from my apartment on 12th in Ladd's Addition. I usually rode my wobbly bike as I was compulsively late. I then carpooled with the supervisor of the new store operation. It was a temp job, but could turn into a full-time if I wanted to work the new store. I thought I might.

I was part of a team that would be building inventory for the new store that they were building in the parking lot of the old. We were given makeshift work stations out in a filthy warehouse.

Behind the action of the Bins, we had our special ops work zone. I got a massive folding table, a chair, a desk lamp. A fresh pallet of totes full of stock would be next to my station every morning. We were to sort and price as many donations as possible so they could stuff the new store to the gills upon grand opening.

At one point during my interview I said, "I like books." And so I was put in charge of pricing books. I got a box of pricing pencils, and enough empty totes to sort the priced books by genre or subject. I would write in pencil the price of the book on the top right of the first page. The book guy at the old store trained me. He was a nice guy, a bit older and intimidating to me. He was very hip and I was very not. His pricing system contained so many exceptions that I gave up trying to remember what he said. I decided to price the things as I saw fit. I saw myself more as a Goodwill shopper than a Goodwill worker. I was a poor bastard. The way I looked at it was, Goodwill was taking things they got for free and making a profit. Under the guise of Non-Profit. I didn't want to help that. It sounded greedy. I was going to price shit for the poor and the cheap. I wanted to help my fellow dumpster divers. My thrift kin. My poor weirdos who still picked pennies off the ground.

The As-Is was where all the items that did not sell at Goodwill stores were dumped in giant rolling bins and sold by the pound. People eventually called it The Bins. Before eBay destroyed the thrift store scene, you would find a lot of junk hound collectors. A lot of punks and weirdos. A lot of families with kids. Russian grandmas and old mechanics. No young pickers making a living off vintage clothes. There were competitive people, mostly older women not afraid to give an elbow for some grandkid clothes.

Now it's all entrepreneur vultures swooping in and swapping stories of profits and cons. Scanning everything with their phones.

There were disabled workers at the Goodwill As-Is. They did all sorts of mostly low-level, menial jobs. There was a guy who swept all day. Giant push broom with the fringe. He wore a metal hard hat, an ancient forties style one with the wide, thick brim and the dome of fluted metal. He also wore steel covers over his boots. I still have never seen anything like his gear. Metal covers that went over the tops of his feet and buckled behind his heels. He walked like a robot horse. You could hear him coming for miles. He was the safest person I have ever seen.

There was a man with static-charged red hair and red mustache. The manager out there was this middle-aged woman who talked to all of them like they were children. Constant stream of NOs and "Not like that!" came out of her mouth. The rest of us, she just gave orders and fake smiles. The break room was always active and always entertaining. My favorite place for sure. There was a woman named Joanne who chatted me up all the time. She would say things like, "Well, I'm glad to talk to such a smart kid. You know, I'm not with them," meaning, the workers with disabilities. She had magnificent tales of being a kidnapped aristocrat. "I don't belong here, you know. My family is royal but they can't find me. I was really something, you know. I was in a movie." One of her friends would call her over and she would try to ignore them. Then she would scream at them and they would cackle and point and enjoy her tantrum.

The manager lady, who was 100% unlikable, opened the freezer one day and let out an almost-scream. She pulled out a small paper bag and held it up in front of the room. "Okay. Who here brought a beer to work? Which one of you brought this beer?" There was a loud gasp in the room. The gasp had only just dissipated when at least four people said CURT very loudly. While pointing and laughing at CURT. Curt threw down his fork and said OH SHUT UP. And everyone laughed and ooooh-ooooohed. The manager lasered in on poor Curt.

"Curt, you can't drink at work. You can't bring a beer to work."

"It was for after! I know that! It was for after! I can have it after!"

"Curt, you need to settle down. You can't bring this into work, Curt. I am putting it in my office and then throwing it away."

"It was for after! Everybody shut up! You all shut up!"

"Curt, you can't bring alcohol to work."

"I am taking it home, it's for home!"

The petty manager motioned for some help and a couple of the men managers came in and led Curt out of the room.

❧

I only stole once. I should be given some credit because the thought crossed my mind every goddamn day. Boxes and boxes of books and records and cassettes and VHS tapes came across my dusty bench. I was frequently reprimanded for being behind and to stop reading the books. One book curled my toes so much that I had to put it behind my belt. That spot in the small of your back where your belt has a bit of slack. Old shoplifter's trick. The one book I nicked and still have was *Erections, Ejaculations, Exhibitions, and General Tales of Ordinary Madness* by Charles Bukowski. I was twenty-one years old and Bukowski was a hero. I still have it, so you know I'm a good person.

It was finally time to move into the brand-spanking-new building. They hauled all the stock I had done into the new store. The book guy who trained me, Jim, opened up a few of my boxes so we could start stocking the shelves.

"Oh, no. No, no, no. Ninety-nine cents for this? Wow, no, no. A dollar ninety-nine for this! No, this should be higher. This is a hardcover, you see that? Oh no, I need to go through these. We are trying to bring in money for this organization, right? I have to look at all this and maybe just redo everything," he said. I shrugged. I helped for a few weeks stocking the shelves and building the store. Excitement was in the air and I enjoyed building a new store. I've always loved being at a job after hours. Closed hours. Locked doors. No public. A few staff wandering about. Half the lights out. Minimum-wage heaven.

They said I could have a full-time job but I would have to work the cash register. I was still abnormally shy and could not deal with being so public. Like the McDonald's job and others before, I said no to the cashier work. So, they gave me until the end of the week and when I still said no I got my last paycheck. I tried to file for unemployment. I was on a three-way call with the unemployment judge and the super at the Goodwill.

"Did you offer Rex a position at the store?"

"Yes I did," said the super, "and he said he didn't want to be a cashier."

"Rex, did you turn down the job?"

"Well, I said I could do anything but work the register. So, I mean, I just turned that down."

"That was the job and he said no," said the super.

"Well, Rex. That's called job refusal and you can't ask for assistance if you are turning down employment. Claim denied and case closed," said the judge or agent or whoever the fuck. They were dead right, of course, and I felt the slapdown. At the same time, they did not realize it was impossible for me to do work in front of so many people, doing math no less, having people look at me or having to talk to people. As a kid, when my mom ordered pizza I would run and hide when the doorbell rang. I couldn't even handle paying the pizza guy when I was younger. "Where's the change?" my mom asked the one time I did.

"There isn't any, I guess."

"What do you mean! You tip him and ask for change back!"

"I don't know what to tip so I gave it all, don't ask me," I cried as I grabbed a slice and went to my room.

A decade or so later, Goodwill made a scandalous splash when it was discovered the CEO was making millions of dollars. How can the head of this massive humanitarian organization be raking in millions? people asked. The name of the place is Goodwill. How can there be greed? I knew it. I smelled it and I knew it. I could look up the CEO woman's name and how much she was pulling in but I don't want to remember those facts. I should have stolen more books.

# Columbia Sportswear

1995–1996

$6/HOUR

To make the 7 a.m. shift I had to catch the 5:45 a.m. bus. I had succumbed to letting the bus shred my waking life and turn me into a brainless drooler. I don't recall a lot of this job as I was walking asleep for most of it. I was in the Quality Control department with a gaggle of older ladies. Was the only male in a department of twelve females. I was well aware that in this warehouse environment I was wearing a pink collar. Our job was to inspect one out of every one hundred boxes or whatever the percentage was, and see if that batch passed specification. Only once do I remember opening a box and finding it filled with oily and ripped-up rain jackets. That was a victorious and momentous day in our department. My boss, a lost soul of a woman who desperately wanted to prove her worth to the higher ups, paraded those greasy garments around to every worker in the warehouse. Our job was to find mistakes where not many were made. Mistakes were validation for our existence.

It was not a hard job whatsoever. You grabbed a box off a pallet. Marked down if it came from Vietnam or China or wherever.

Cut the box open. Pulled out a jacket or fleece bullshit thing and checked all the stitching and pockets. You measured everything to a list of specs. Sleeve length. Collar width. Did the zipper work? Was the hood easy to fold back up? Did the button color match the fabric color? It was so easy and utterly pointless that it wounded my brain. My head was screaming FEED ME FEED ME. I said, do you remember money, brain? It's what this whole world is about. We can read on our lunch break.

The forklift guys were all white, mostly young redneck jock types. The warehouse was by a river, or a slough to be more exact. When the slough was high, tiny frogs would swarm the warehouse. I thought it was fantastic. I had never seen much frog action, being from the desert. They were little green ones, mostly long toothpick legs. The forklift boys competed over who could run over the most frogs. Enough said.

One of these guys asked me the question (which to this day still makes me cringe), "What kind of music do you listen to, man?" Two things about this question. 1. My mind immediately snaps back into its turtle shell and puts out the I DON'T KNOW sign on its sealed entrance. 2. Often when people ask this they are trying to open you up for a chance to knock you down a peg. No matter what answer you give they will stomp on it and make you feel millions of dollars in shame.

"I don't know," I said while not making eye contact. At the time I was heavy into Lightnin' Hopkins, Billie Holiday, Louis Armstrong and His Hot Five. Bob Dylan. Nick Drake. These were not obscure artists by any means, but I assumed he would not know them. And that would surely give him the chance to call me smart or faggy. Which in the warehouse world was like a swift kick in the balls. When men talk to each other and someone gets called smart, you know that one is going to get his ass beat.

"C'mon, man. What do you mean? You know what music you like. Tell me."

"Yeah, I dunno. Everything, I guess." I continued the no eye contact. His brother forklift drivers were looking me up and down. I had longish hair, patched-up thrift jeans, black Nikes I had duct taped together till I could afford new shoes. I was sweating in my sweatshirt.

"Everything?! Really? What, am I not cool enough to know what you're listening to? Is that it? You think you know something I don't, right? Just tell me a name, man. I'm not gonna bite. Just tell me the name of one band." He nearly snarled all this. His face was flushed and he had half-fists in his hands.

His supervisor was an older ginger who I actually thought was cool. He had the uncanny ability of always knowing what time it was. He didn't wear a watch. People tested him all the time: "Okay, what time is it?" and he would look at the ceiling, curl one of his eyes and say, "Hmmmm, seems like two-fifteen." And he would be right. Every time. I've never met anyone with that skill since.

"Okay, cool it. Leave the kid alone," time keeper said.

"He won't answer me! I'm just trying to talk to him!"

"Yeah, and he answered like he wanted to. Let it go."

"I want him to answer my question. Why won't he do that?!"

"Leave it alone. Let's get back to work, guys. That's enough."

I was very careful not to be caught alone with that guy. Going to the bathroom was akin to a mission behind enemy lines for me. If that guy caught me alone I would probably have gotten my ass kicked. Maybe that would have helped me suggest a few albums for him. Maybe if you get beat up at work you get to take a few days off. I would have taken that deal. Or at least a long lunch.

| 1 Wages, tips, other comp. | 2 Federal income tax withheld |
|---|---|
| 4059.57 | 399.93 |
| 3 Social security wages | 4 Social security tax withheld |
| 4059.57 | 251.69 |
| 5 Medicare wages and tips | 6 Medicare tax withheld |
| 4059.57 | 58.86 |

| a Control Number | Dept. | Corp. | Employer use only |
|---|---|---|---|
| 005962 SZS | 541031 | T | 419 |

c Employer's name, address, and ZIP code

**COLUMBIA SPORTSWEAR CO
6603 NORTH BALTIMORE
PORTLAND OR 97203**

**Batch #00201**

| b Employer's FED ID number | d Employee's SSA |
|---|---|
| 93-0498284 | |
| 7 Social security tips | 8 Allocated tips |
| 9 Advance EIC payment | 10 Dependent care benefits |
| 11 Nonqualified plans | 12 Benefits included in box 1 |
| 13 See instrs. for box 13 | 14 Other |

| 15 Stat emp. | Deceased | Pension plan | Legal rep. | Hshld. emp. | Deferred comp. |
|---|---|---|---|---|---|

e/f Employee's name, address and ZIP code

**REX MARSHALL
.PT 5
PORTLAND,OR 97214**

| 16 State | Employer's state ID | 17 State wages, tips, etc. |
|---|---|---|
| OR | 177103 2 | 4059.57 |
| 18 State income tax | | 19 Locality name |
| 248.03 | | |
| 20 Local wages, tips, etc. | | 21 Local income tax |

**Employee Reference Copy
W-2 Wage and Tax Statement 1996**
Copy C for Employee's Records. OMB No. 1545-0008

# AMF Pro 300 Bowling Lanes

1996

$5/HOUR

I watched cars in the parking lot. I had a fake police badge pinned to my ratty blue nylon hooded parka. I patrolled the downstairs garage and the upstairs lot. I spent most of my time leaning against a dented metal railing and reading paperback books by the dumpster.

My girlfriend worked in the kitchen. She was vegetarian but didn't mind cooking hamburgers. She would sneak out massive custom burgers to me. Burgers with bacon and mushrooms. Burgers with chicken strips on top of beef. Bowls of bacon and fries. I ate like a king, standing by my dumpster in the rain. Free food is the way to my heart.

A craggly old guy worked behind the pins as the mechanic. Always pointing at shit with his cigarette hand. He had never left the seventies, kind of a biker vibe. I liked him and was a little afraid of him. They had him train me on the machines, the contraptions that drop and clear the pins. There were twelve lanes at the Pro 300. And six ball returns. The few hours I spent back there training were chaos. Packed house, ten lanes being used. Something always breaking and constant emergencies.

"Okay, lane six always jams after four rounds and it's because it's not registering balls when they hit the back board—which triggers the machine to drop and clasp, right? So you have to reach up and in and pull that board back. That's the easy way. Ten doesn't read splits so you have to stick this pole in there to hit the switch. See that? Got it—good." Bells and alarms rang when problems happened. The bowlers couldn't see you, but you could hear them. "C'mon, man, where's my ball? I want my money back, this lane is shit!"

The mechanic called in sick one day and I was drafted as mechanic for the day. Was a cold light snow-falling day. I remember a small window on the side back there that didn't close all the way. Snow gently blew in. I had a mug of hot tea and looked out at a football field as snow fell. Alarm bells started ringing like mad. It was a full assault. Four lanes crashed. Ring ring ring. I rushed over to one, saw that the ball had not hit hard enough to reset the pin drop. Easy. Slap the ball to the ball return gutter. Pull back the board until the trigger clicked.

Another lane had a pin stuck sideways in the mechanism and I hated it but I had to reach in there and claw it out. The mechanic's words echoed in my head: "Right here—this will break your arm if you trigger it and you're in there!" I took a broom handle and knocked it in there and flipped the pin out. Another lane had a pin fly out onto the lane. I had to step out onto the lanes, jump from gutter to gutter, and grab the dumb thing. I still had two lanes down. I tried heroically to fix one but my three hours of training had not given me the trick to this one. Then Ed, the sweet old fella who had worked there for twenty years, came waltzing in. He was always cleanly dressed and was a father figure type of good man. "Hey young man, how we doing back here?"

"I have no clue how to fix that one. I know it's been twenty minutes. I can't do it."

Ed smiled a kind smile and reached for a metal rod that I hadn't noticed leaning in the corner. He grabbed with both hands and jammed it at an angle into the pin dropper. Something clicked and whirred and the machine came back to life. "Don't tell anybody I know how to do this, kid. Then they'll make me do more work!"

It was summer and I stood out front in my bowling alley polo shirt with my fake badge.  I was dreaming of my lunch break, leaning against the rock façade back on my parking lot shift. A guy zipped up on his mountain bike and leaned it against the opposite rock façade. "Keep an eye on my bike," he said. I should have said no but I nodded. He was inside for maybe five minutes before another guy came out of the bowling alley and jumped on the damn bike.

I said very lamely, "Hey, that's not yours!" as he took off. He smirked at me. I chased for a bit as it fully dawned on me that the bowling alley was on top of a hill. He was a rocket I didn't have hope of catching.

As I was running back, the guy was out front foaming at the mouth. He came at me.

"Hey, where's my bike, kid? You tell me where my bike is!"

"Yeah, a guy jumped on it and took off. I tried to chase him. I'll go call the cops."

"No, man, listen, you need to get me back my bike. I don't care where—you need to get it. We are gonna go get it, right? You're coming with me to find it."

I was confused and I said NO as I got by him and went inside. I went behind the desk to my manager's office. I forget his name, but let's say we call him Turtle. Turtle was lamely sitting at his desk in his office and I was explaining what went down. The guy had followed me in. He cut me off.

"Hey, look, I want to go look for my bike and I want this kid to come with me to help," bike guy said.

Turtle said, "Oh, we should call the cops," with quivering lips.

"No. No cops. I'm taking the kid. You good with that?"

And Turtle, as I was looking into his eyes with my terrified horrified begging eyes, said,

"Oh, uh, well, sure... that seems okay with me. You just check back here after, right, Rex?"

The guy grabbed me by the back of my arm and led me back outside.

This guy had a hold of my arm and he said through his teeth, "Look, fucker, I had two hundred dollars of crystal on that bike. You know I did. You are gunna get your friend to give it back to me. I don't give a fuck if we walk all over the fucking city tonight. I don't care if you say you didn't do it. You are gunna get it back to me. Start walking."

"I... I don't know where to go. I didn't do it. I ran after him."

"Yeah, bullshit. Start walking."

I stopped and shook free of his hand. "I can't. I'm not going. I don't know where to go. I can't do this." I was impressed that I was not crying. I was on the edge, but my voice was almost steady.

Then a seriously weird thing occurred. As I was planting my feet and refusing to step any further, my vision went blurry, as if something fast had run right in front of me. Why was my head swiveling? Then it happened again. Whoosh. My head or maybe my eyes were just out of control. I saw his arm fall back to his side and I understood. He had punched me twice. There was no pain, and I did not even get a bruise or black eye later. I ran inside and bust into tears as soon as the air conditioning hit my face. Turtle popped out of his office. I was trying to get out of sight quick so I could cry. "Rex, you're back already?"

"He punched me in the face! I shouldn't have gone with him."

Turtle made a frog face and let me into his office. He was clearly grossed out the way men are when they see another male cry. He called the cops. Ed the father figure gave me ice wrapped in a dish cloth. He hated my crying, but with sympathy. The cops, they hated my crying even more. They conveyed the feeling they thought I was a true loser for not fighting a grown adult drug dealer.

Months went by. I didn't come to work for a week, and seriously thought of never coming back. But money. And my hamburger-smuggling girlfriend. I tried to find excuses to stay inside all day as it was a hot one. I was cleaning bowling shoes when I saw a guy in aviators come in and head for the arcade room. My hackles went up. I tiptoed past the arcade and confirmed it was the guy. I went into the small diner where my girlfriend worked. I could hear the druggie playing pinball through the wall. I talked to Ed but didn't say anything about it. Maybe the guy is just playing the game on a hot day. He can't be here for me. There's no way someone would do that.

I was not thinking strategically when, maybe an hour later, I decided to go outside. I went out through a side door that locked from the outside automatically. And it was far from the front door. I sauntered out and stared at the street when the guy came out the front door. He saw me and moved towards me quick. I had cut myself off from the bowling alley. There were no windows so no one could see me. He was on me in no time.

"Hey faggot, yeah, I didn't forget. You owe me two hundred. I didn't forget. I'm gunna fucking kill you right here. You owe me two hundred bucks. You fuck. Let's go. Let's go get your money. You owe me."

"I didn't steal your bike. I didn't. I told you," I said.

"Fuck you. I am going to fuck you up. I can follow you home and fucking kill you. I'm gonna be here everyday, faggot." And he kicked me so very hard between the legs.

Then, a miracle occurred. A stinky, homeless hunk of a miracle. His name was Ron.

The scene of the miracle was Powell Blvd, the year 1996. Powell is a busy main street in Portland. The Pro 300 was across from a bottom-rung strip club and a tarnished Motel 6 where hookers conspicuously worked. There was a lot of drug activity and drunks. Quite a few neighborhood homeless people. I was friends with a few of these guys. I would get off work and walk around with them. Buy them hamburgers at McDonald's. Wild Bill was my favorite. He wore a groovy Western-style hat and cowboy boots. He had a sweet black dog he loved so much. He lived under the concrete lip of the bowling alley's foundation where it intersected the underground parking zone. Strange building fluke or bad design. The Pro 300 owners let him do it, which I thought was awesome. He had built a wall from scrap wood and made a cozy cliff den dwelling under there. The bowling alley let him plug an extension cord into an outlet in the lower parking lot. He had a heater and a little TV. Wild Bill had a severe limp, courtesy of a Bouncing Betty in Vietnam. After I got comfortable with him, I asked why he lived on the street.

"I was out on patrol and stepped on a mine. Just heard a soft click. Almost lost this leg. That got me a ticket home, but I can't do shit with it. I get a disability check for about five hundred bucks. If I get a job, I'm ineligible for disability. I can't work that much anyway 'cause I can't stand too long. Anyway, if I work I lose my checks and if I keep my checks I can't afford to get a place. So there ya go."

There was a guy named Chucky I cruised with a couple times. Chucky was a wino of the old times. He was always drunk-drunk. Always blitzed. I snuck him burgers and fries. He would start eating and be thankful and suddenly drop the food in the street and walk off like he was late for an appointment. I thought he was sad but fantastic. He told stories. He was an entertainer. He would walk up to people in the McDonald's drive-thru and get them to order food for us. He always shared. I rarely accepted 'cause I had a job. He told me to keep food in my pocket 'cause you never know. Once in the park there on Powell and 26th he was checking in on some bum, and this guy who was face down in his sleeping bag rolled over and sat up pointing a snub-nose at us. It was matte black and ugly. Then he cackled like the best joke had been told. Chucky was spooked and maybe upset but just lightly slapped the guy on the head. You can't really get mad at someone holding a gun. Street smarts 101.

There was another guy who was all sketch. I gave him a winter jacket and a pair of gloves. Next time I saw him he had cut the fingers off the gloves. I brought a bag of hamburgers and sat with him and a couple other street guys. "Hey kid, thanks for the food, man, this is great. Hey, you look strong, right? You work out? You want to get some workout gear, like a bench and weights and stuff? There's some at my buddy's house. We just have to go over there and help ourselves. Probably better to do it at night. Whaddya say?"

And last but not least, my miracle angel bum Ron. Ron was a laid-off lumberjack from the coast. The story I pieced together was that he got canned, spiraled, and hit the booze hard, then his wife divorced him and took the house and car and slammed him with a huge alimony. "The second I get a job, she gets five of every ten I make. So, I'm just off the radar a bit so I'm not her honey pot." Ron was a real sweet guy. He was always checking up on the older guys out on the street. He had a yellow ten-speed. He smelled like b.o., was well-muscled, dirty, and had heart. He was one of those men who could be either twenty-five or forty-five.

Back to the scene. The meth head is in my face after kicking me swiftly and decisively in the nuts. My brain was as smashed as my balls. I did not know how to fight whatsoever. I had been hit many times in my life, but always found an escape. I was now fantastically boxed in. There is fight and there is flight, and then there is freeze, which is where I was.

Out of nowhere, Ron the angel rode up and skidded his ten-speed between me and the guy who possibly just made me infertile.

I did not make a sound or fall to the ground when he field-kicked his sneaker into my goal. I clenched my jaw and chewed on the stars I saw.

"Hey, what the hell! You can't kick this kid! Back off," Ron said.

"He stole my shit, man. He owes me," said the tweaker.

"What shit?"

"My bike, man. My stash."

"Naw, naw. This kid doesn't even do drugs. He works here. He doesn't even drink. He didn't steal your shit. Back off," said Ron.

"Fuck you. This fuck owes me. I'm gunna follow you home and kill you. I'll be here and you won't expect it. And I'll follow you home and kill you."

"Hey! Get out of here before I fuck you up, man. You have to get through me to get him and that ain't happening. Get the fuck out of here," Ron shouted and pointed to where the guy should fuck off to. The tweaker walked backwards, still spewing a torrent of terrible promises. When he was out of sight I fell back against the wall of the bowling alley.

"You alright, kid? He get you good?"

"Yeah, he did. I feel sick."

"But you didn't show him that. That's real good! That's how you do it out here. You don't show how they hurt you. Fuck that guy. You good?"

"I'm going to go inside and they will probably call the cops. I can't believe you showed up like that. You saved me. I can't believe it. Thank you. I can't believe it."

"Oh shit, that guy was a loser. Cops? I better take off. Take it easy, kid." My stinky miracle, my homeless angel rode off and I never saw him again.

Cops didn't do anything except listen to my story, and even though the guy had stalked me and this was the second time he had assaulted me, they said there wasn't much to do. "Call us if he shows up again," they said and gave me a business card. Then Turtle the worthless boss shrugged his shoulders at me. I guess the cops needed to see a knife sticking out of my side. I quit.

# OFFICE DEPOT

1996–97
$5.50/HOUR

John Hook was a Vietnam vet who had a filthy mouth and was the spitting image of Popeye except for his Coke-bottle-thick eyeglasses. He tucked in his Depot blue polo and swore by his black velcro back brace. He had one of those up-to-no-good laughs. To sum it up simply, I would say he was a dirty old man of the best sort. I hung out with him at his apartment after work a couple times. He drank High Life and the stories flowed out. The kind of guy who was still talking as you backed out of the door to exit. I wish I remembered any of the tales. Most were about hookers and war.

I was a Stocker, or "Stockboy" to those who talked down. I refilled and straightened shelves, hung merch on hooks, and had to do inventory. I swept floors, I took out trash. I avoided the cash register, of course. I was still too shy and also deathly afraid of money math. They tried to train me but I dodged. I pretended to forget everything. Sorry, team, my memory is not great. Not my fault I'm in a long line of deficient ancestors. The cash register is for the gifted!

The hellish part of my job was carting furniture out to cars. Office Depot wasn't just pens and printer ink. We had executive credenzas. CEO-level leather office chairs. Bookcases. Boxes of computer paper. Gallon jugs of water. My name would project over the intercom all the damn time. "Rex to the front." I would cinch up the velcro on my lumbar support back brace and head up to the registers to see what monster waited for me.

Seven times out of ten, the part that was both most enjoyable and top-ranked annoying was explaining to the customer that the eight-foot desk was not going to fit in their Honda Civic. Since retail is about bowing down to your Lord Customer, one had to do this without telling them they were dumb. John Hook, however, had his own script. He did not believe the customer was always right and would tell it to their faces. He would wheel something out on a cart, take a look at their tiny, fuel-efficient two-seater, and just cackle out loud, then walk back inside without saying a word. The customer would run after him. John would walk up to the front manager, and with the customer there stomping their feet he would say, "This laaaady bought an eight-foot desk and has a four-foot economy car. What am I supposed to do about it? Sell her a bigger car? Hah!"

Office Depot was one of the first chain stores to store their overstock on industrial shelves above the merchandise out on the floor. Home Depot was the business that revolutionized this. Well, to the best of my knowledge. I care that little about retail history to not verify this. Anyway, a biz saves on overhead by not having to rent a space to keep the back stock. Combine the store and the warehouse under one roof. Just put it way on top, and pull it down as needed.

The monsters. The Executive Chairs. The beasts were five feet tall, three feet wide, weighed eighty pounds. There was one forklift in the place and only the jock night crew used it when the store was closed. When a customer pulled a ticket for an Executive Chair you just groaned and got ready for hurt. We cussed and cursed when someone bought one of those beasts. We had rolling ladders—more like a set of stairs with a railing on each side. John showed me the trick to getting one of these chairs down. Still, I almost died. I shudder even thirty years later.

You had to hike to the top step of the ladder and grab the fridge-sized box and shake it back and forth and pull it towards you. Then, you could pull it forward so it rested on the edge of the top ladder rail. What you had to do was get it to sit on the rail while you slowly walked it down. As it was pressing full gravity-style against your chest. That way you didn't have to pick it up, you just had to slow its fall as you stepped backwards down the ladder. You would get into position by putting the side of your face and neck and shoulder against the bottom of this giant, heavy box. You bent your knees and tried to weld them to the steps. When you knocked the box forward, its weight would hit you hard. It wanted to crush you to death. Both of your wrists would be smashed and straining against the cardboard box. If you lost hold of the railing, you would probably lose an arm or hand or maybe the inertia of the two-hundred-pound box would knock your head right off. The soles of my cheap sneakers and my sweaty palms squeaked against the gravity of this made-in-China pleather beast.

It wasn't over when your feet hit the concrete floor. Now you had to get the monster off your neck and chest and onto the ground without dropping it. If you dropped it, the rolling base would break a wheel, or bend, and then you would have to climb up and get another. This was where you hoped you had another Stocker next to you. Sometimes you didn't, and you just kinda had to hunch down to your knees and then kinda lay down on your ass with the chair in your lap. In other words, I used my own body, my skinny beans-and-rice-and-ramen-fueled non-muscle body, to buffer the fall of this Executive Chair. Again, let's recall how much I made. $6.00 an hour.

This was the job where hyper-anger really flared up in me. I say "hyper" because I was. I had so much energy. I was twenty-two. When you're chained to a dead-end job, every pointless shift cranks the generator of your anger and hatred of the job thing. I was hanging ballpoint pens on hooks, organizing toner cartridges, stocking highlighters, and stacking copy paper. I was not a rich kid. I had to get my card in that clock and punch it. I wanted to punch everything else. I had lists of things to do. I wanted to write, I wanted to read. I wanted to play guitar, learn piano, speak Latin, try once again to paint, attempt fishing, take kung fu lessons. I wanted a thick, boxy car. I wanted to drive till the road ended, then jump out and walk till I hit the horizon. But I had to eat my dreams and tuck in my blue Office Depot polo.

Mostly I think I just wanted my time to be my time. I wanted to never hear an alarm clock again. My eyes would open and I would kick out of the sheets only when I felt like the time was right. Make some coffee, look at the paper. Sit in the sun if it was sunny, or plop on the couch and stare if it was rainy. I would make some breakfast and read a book or maybe just go back to fucking bed and waste a day. In other words, do whatever or do nothing whenever I chose. I was pissed for all of my twenties and most of my thirties. About money and the world I couldn't change. At this point in my life, as I write this, the machine has finally ground me down and I don't kick and drive myself nuts so much anymore. I don't make a ton but I've been smart about money and my overhead. I have a solid handful of side hustles.  I still eat beans, rice, and I've upgraded from Top Ramen. I can't complain about where I'm at in the workforce. Even so here I am, decades later, still scheming and dreaming to have my time be my own.

## No Tax

Office Depot is where I worked with the one and only person I have ever met, and probably will ever meet, who stopped paying taxes and did all the steps to stop from ever having to. He was an old dodger, mid sixties?, a Mr. Burns character but not as smart. He was Anti-everything, which I used to love to listen to. Anti-Government was a topic that got him fired up.

"Do you even pay attention to how much they take in taxes from you? Yeah yeah, where does it go? You know it's not the law to pay taxes right? Yeah. It's not mandatory. They can't make you, but nobody knows! I haven't paid in decades. I'm almost done with the battle, too. I fought these leeches for years. They said they're taking away my social security number. Fine! Take it! What do I get from that anyway? Not close to what they're taking, that's what. So yeah, I went through the whole process and I will get all the money I work for, every check, not one cent grabbed by Uncle Sam, yeah yeah!"

And there was the swing shift crew at Office Depot. Their boss was a short wannabe military guy who looked a lot like Ron Howard. He had a crisp voice and was very proud. Typical rooster of a man. His evening crew were a bunch of guys who thought they were NFL players. They competed over who did the most unboxing and shelving. Who unloaded the most boxes from the trucks. Lots of high fives and even ass slapping. This crew would take showers with each other if Office Depot had showers.

I would sit outside for my strict thirty minute lunch breaks. Sheridan Grocery was next door and I would buy whatever was cheapest. Sit on the side of the building. Next to my bike because once someone stole the seat off it and I had to ride the three miles home without it. When it was rainy I sat in the miserable break room. Maybe a ten-by-ten square, dingy back room with large gray tables. Filthy microwave on the dusty counter. Drafty chicken-wire glass windows. I would sit in the corner with my budget lunch and read. Then the night crew would show up and bomb my peace. I was always guaranteed my fifteen minutes of lame.

"Hey college boy, what are you reading now?" That was the head stud. His name was Danny or Billy or Tony. He actually called me college boy. At that time I had taken a handful of classes at Portland Community College. I was putting myself through college and couldn't afford a full course load. I didn't really have parents. I still had no degree goals or career sights. I could only see bills on my horizon. Anyway, *college boy* was because I had a fucking book. It was probably Chandler or Bukowski or Stephen King. Highfalutin ivory tower material only.

That one with the normal name, he was the uber-jock and kind of the leader of the pack. He did get real with me once, I remember. "So you going to college and probably getting out of here one day, right?" he asked. "I mean, I hope I get out of here, yeah. I can't stay here," I said. "Yeah. That's cool, man. I don't think I ever read a book. I gotta work and I'm good at this job. I gotta, like, do real good and maybe I'll get a raise. This is it for guys like me, man. You're lucky you're smart, dude."

I rode my mountain bike up and down Grand Avenue and somehow landed a bellboy job at the Holiday Inn. I was thrilled. I remember Office Depot tried to talk me out of quitting. Offered me a raise that was not even close to the new bellboy wage I would nab. A couple of coworkers talked in awe of how much more I would make. I was confused. Why don't you go look for another job? Why stay? When you have a job it's near impossible to find the time, much less the energy, to look for another. I knew you could never jump off a train until you saw another one coming. It's easy to get complacent in a place and routine. I was young and dumb but I knew I didn't want to wither and die in an Office Depot.

I went back there in 2017 looking for some annoying tech thing, an adapter or something. I had a coupon for 20% off. The whole store was different. Gutted and remodeled. Felt like hell in there. Stifling. Bright. Still the cheap overpriced furniture and ergonomic heavy chairs made out of plastic 'n' pleather. I looked at the few employees in there. They looked simultaneously haggard and young.

A guy came out of the back office and I immediately recognized the way he walked. It was Michael, the assistant manager from 1996. Still uptight and bossy. Still chewing on his bottom lip and completely phony. He would run to the boss and tattle on everyone for the smallest things. Maybe he had never once thought to look for another train. I thought about saying, "Hi, Michael! I hope they gave you a raise or two for your dedication. Love the new polo shirt uniform. I hope they pay for your coffin. They should sell coffins at Office Depot. Tell that to your boss!"

# RANDOM DEPOT MEMORIES

Once a man tapped me on the shoulder and said, "Excuse me, is your name Rex? 'Cause mine is, too! I kept hearing my name over the system and I was so confused, and then I saw you and, well, here we are!" I've only met five or six in my life. I asked him if he got picked on as a kid. He confirmed it was hell to grow up Rex.

Decades and lifetimes later, after a rare heavy snow night, I walked around my neighborhood enjoying the powder and came upon my name written in the snow at the top of the street. I was alarmed. Who is out to kill me? Later I drove by that house and saw that the Office Depot Rex lives there. He's still there. I've never talked to him. Isn't that strange? I feel it's too weird that I remember him. It's a secret I have with my street that has yet to be leaked.

Finding the right printer ink for every model of computer printer back then was a tedious and demanding chore. Color printers were all the rage. I hated the office supplies. Every office person who had to pick them up knew they were office gophers on the bottom rung. They were rarely thrilled and not easy to please.

We sold computers and some were set up as working displays. One of them had a bunch of games loaded. *DOOM* was a game that had just come out. I snuck over there multiple times every shift. It was a hand with a gun and you just walked through buildings and shot aliens. The sounds were the best, all grunts and shots and heavy thumping footsteps.

---

OMB No. 1545-0008

CORRECTED

| a Control number | 1 Wages, tips, other compensation | 2 Federal income tax withheld |
|---|---|---|
| 39096 | 6147.63 | 540.50 |
| | 3 Social security wages | 4 Social security tax withheld |
| This information is being furnished to the Internal Revenue Service. If you are required to file a tax return, a negligence penalty or other sanction may be imposed on you if this income is taxable and you fail to report it. | 6147.63 | 381.15 |
| | 5 Medicare wages and tips | 6 Medicare tax withheld |
| | 6147.63 | 89.14 |
| | (See Notice On Back) | |

c Employer's name, address, and ZIP code

OFFICE DEPOT
2200 OLD GERMANTOWN ROAD
DELRAY BEACH, FL          33445

| 7 Social security tips | 8 Allocated tips | 9 Advance EIC payment |
|---|---|---|
| .00 | .00 | .00 |
| 10 Dependent care benefits | 11 Nonqualified plans | 12 Benefits included in Box 1 |
| .00 | .00 | .00 |

| b Employer's identification number | d Employee's social security number |
|---|---|
| 592663954 | |

| 13 See instrs. for Box 13 | 14 Other |
|---|---|

e Employee's name, address, and ZIP code

REX K MARSHALL
              #9
PORTLAND   OR
97202

| 15 Statutory employee | Deceased | Pension plan | Legal rep. | Hshld. emp. | Subtotal | Deferred compensation |
|---|---|---|---|---|---|---|

| 1996 | 16 State | Employer's state I.D. No. | 17 State wages, tips, etc. |
|---|---|---|---|
| W-2 Wage and Tax Statement | OR | 399281-6 | 6147.63 |

| 18 State income tax | 19 Locality name |
|---|---|
| 342.12 | |

Copy C For EMPLOYEE'S RECORDS

| 20 Local wages, tips, etc. | 21 Local income tax |
|---|---|
| .00 | .00 |

Department of the Treasury—Internal Revenue Service

---

OMB No. 1545-0008

| a Control number | 1 Wages, tips, other compensation | 2 Federal income tax withheld |
|---|---|---|
| 40558 | 4642.14 | 356.46 |
| | 3 Social security wages | 4 Social security tax withheld |
| | 4642.14 | 287.81 |
| | 5 Medicare wages and tips | 6 Medicare tax withheld |
| | 4642.14 | 67.31 |
| | This information is being furnished to the Internal Revenue Service. | |

c Employer's name, address, and ZIP code

OFFICE DEPOT INC.
2200 OLD GERMANTOWN ROAD
DELRAY BEACH, FL          33445

| 7 Social security tips | 8 Allocated tips | 9 Advance EIC payment |
|---|---|---|
| .00 | .00 | .00 |
| 10 Dependent care benefits | 11 Nonqualified plans | 12 Benefits included in Box 1 |
| .00 | .00 | .00 |

| b Employer's identification number | d Employee's social security number |
|---|---|
| 592663954 | |

| 13 See instrs. for Box 13 | 14 Other |
|---|---|

e Employee's name, address, and ZIP code

REX K MARSHALL
       SE 26 #9
PORTLAND   OR
97202

| 15 Statutory employee | Deceased | Pension plan | Legal rep. | Hshld. emp. | Subtotal | Deferred compensation |
|---|---|---|---|---|---|---|

| 1997 | 16 State | Employer's state I.D. No. | 17 State wages, tips, etc. |
|---|---|---|---|
| W-2 Wage and Tax Statement | OR | 399281-6 | 4642.14 |

| 18 State income tax | 19 Locality name |
|---|---|
| 241.79 | |

Copy B To Be Filed With Employee's FEDERAL Tax Return          16-0331690

| 20 Local wages, tips, etc. | 21 Local income tax |
|---|---|
| .00 | .00 |

Department of the Treasury—Internal Revenue Service

# Holiday Inn Portland, Convention Center

1997–98
$6.25/hour

Hotels are really all about sex and it was the horniest job I've ever had. I brought hair dryers to the rooms of women who were traveling alone. I would bring an ironing board, be asked to step inside and set it up as they sat on the bed in a skirt and slowly pulled their hose off. One woman, attending a convention for the weekend, had me deliver things to her room multiple times. Each time she leaned against the door frame and asked me questions in a husky voice. Each time she wore a blouse that was a bit more open. I brought up a hair dryer and she wore a sheer robe that hid nothing and her eyes went up and conspicuously down my body. I was a shy kid. I ran away, went to the break room. Kicked the snack machine till it gave me free Famous Amos.

I spent the majority of my thirty-five hours a week at this job hiding from work. I always had a paperback book in my back pocket, or hidden somewhere in the hotel. I would sit out on one of the fire escapes and read. I had a walkie-talkie I had to keep an ear on. I would wait until the second or third time I heard my name. I could also ignore it and play dumb. I played dumb so often that they believed I was dumb. I became the dumb one and had only myself to blame. I could not counter that I was dumb, that I was taking all the college courses I could afford because that would blow my slacker cover. That I read two or more books a week back then. So yeah, I embraced the dumb and didn't work hard whatsoever. I wasn't making enough money to be smart for these people. No one who stayed at the Holiday Inn were big tippers. Even less reason to be on my toes. I was on my ass—my dumb ass—making minimum wage, stealing bread and food from the kitchen, filling my pockets with coffee beans.

All the employees were fucking. They were gross and unattractive mostly, but I was jealous and felt like a boy constantly looking over the fence to see what the busy neighbors were up to. There were parking lot blow jobs, orgies, hints of bosses cheating on their wives with hostesses. Someone talked about sucking someone's foot. I went to the apartment of a front desk guy one night. It was kinda fun but not really. Maybe five people sitting on a couch, talking about whatever dumbness was popular. I was in the kitchen and Morgan (a front desk guy, short and very cocky) comes up really fast and gives me a handshake with a condom in it. "Here, wrap your dick and fuck Kristy. She needs to get stuffed, she just broke up with her lame dude. Fuck that girl! Don't blow it!" He then pushed me in the living room. I did indeed blow it. I did not want to accept the mission. I was a walking hard-on and Kristy was cute, but my shyness was more powerful than all of my mighty boners. I had never really talked to her, how the hell could I fuck her. Kristy gazed at me, sat very close and touched her leg to my leg. She had thrown back a few Bartles & Jaymes. I gave her a smudge of a hug and left. The real nail in the condom was knowing that all of the Convention Center Holiday Inn would be waiting and expecting to hear all about our fucking. I couldn't even.

The Cubans were a combo meal of thrill and terror. One of them was a house keeper, one a prep cook. I would get talked at for hours by these guys and have no idea what they were saying. But I felt like we were pals. We laughed a lot. Mostly I laughed. Those guys were on a level I could only gawk at. So much energy. So alive.

One night there was a fashion show upstairs in the ballroom. A lot of hair and makeup, swishy hip traffic in the elevators. I went up to the kitchen, hoping to steal my usual soup and bread. Was a ghost town up there. No one around. I grabbed some bread. I heard a noise around the corner. The fashion show was put together with movable walls, kinda like giant cubicle partitions that could be moved around to make the space bigger or smaller or whatever. The walls had seams which were probably an inch wide. So it happened that a gap in one of the walls happened to be in the middle of the models' dressing room. Where the Cubans were standing all over each other, peeking through and trying to be quiet.

The Cubans were huddled around one of the gaps with their hands cupping over the sides of their eyes. They hushly waved me over. "Hey, hey! Shhh. Okay. Hahaha. Shh! Be quiet, okay!" The Cook was standing on his tiptoes and the Housekeeper was squatting, both cupping their eyes over a seam. The Cook's hand was crawling around under his apron. He saw me and turned away from me. His back was to me, but I could tell he was zipping up. The Housekeeper waved me over.

"Check it out! My friend! Shh, be quiet. Come here!" he said with quiet exclamations.

They parted and gave me room. The Housekeeper held his finger to his mouth. Shhhhsh. He grabbed me by the shoulder and mimed for me to look through the gap. I saw a woman in there take off her top. She had a purple bra on. She then put on another top, adjusted her hair, and walked out. Another strolled in and pulled off her skirt as she sat down in a cheap office chair. Both were drinking from white paper cups and hung out in the way only the extremely bored do.

I was boiling with hormones and even I did not get a rise out of this peep. I grew up in Vegas, guys. I saw showgirls and naked women before I could walk. I looked through the hole in the wall for a couple minutes and shrugged at the Cubans, using my limited body language to say, "Uh, yeah, guys, pretty cool." I looked at the kitchen Cuban and he was wiping his pants with his dish towel. A saucer-sized wet spot was unhidable. The Housekeeper whispered, "It's mayo-naise. Mayo-naise! Haha! Man!" I used my limited miming skills to say without words, "Haha, I believe you," and I slapped one of them on the back like guys do and got out of there. As I stepped back through the kitchen, one of the front desk guys was walking through. "Hey, where is everybody up here? We've had food orders waiting for like thirty minutes! Are they over there?" "Uh, yeah, they're around the, uh, corner," I said and got the hell out of there.

A few days after the Christmas party that year, everyone was very subdued. Something had changed. Morgan was a squat, short guy with the clichéd Napoleon complex who thought he was *Top Gun* because he could type on the computer fast. He did have Tom Cruise hair, which he fingered a lot. He worked at the biggest hotel in Missoula or Boise or some other not-braggable city. He was the front desk guy who tried to get me to bang the office girl. He had a foursome with some of the banquet/bar crew and gloated constantly. "Hey Morgan, how was the party? Where is everybody today? Seems like no one is working Banquet."

"It wasn't good at all. All Banquet people are off. Upstairs is shut down. Some terrible shit went down. You know Angelica, the hostess upstairs? Jose from the kitchen tried to rape her at the party. He was beyond wasted and just went nuts. He had her locked inside the bathroom. Her clothes were all ripped. Someone found him and it took a bunch of them to tackle him and get him off her. He went to jail, she went to the hospital."

Jose was the mayonnaise Cuban from the kitchen. He had a wife and two kids. Who were at the party, I think. Angelica was one of the few who was genuine and nice to chat with. A few weeks after Christmas, I saw her come in and quietly pick up her final check. She was wearing a baseball hat pulled low over her eyes like she had something to hide. Everyone working got quiet and there was no fucking orgy talk for once. I felt for her. I hope she sued the piss out of all the managers and the company.

## Bomb Threat

My Holiday Inn was directly across the street from the Convention Center. Every city has these black holes in the center, sucking in the worst out-of-towners and dumbest events. Summers were peak season for all that garbage. The front desk got me through my walkie-talkie, told me to come to the lobby ASAP.

There were a couple of cops down there talking to the desk staff. Rodney the manager came over to me. "Okay, a bomb threat was called in. To the Convention Center. It sounds real. I need you to help keep people away from the downstairs parking. The police have closed the street down there and want everyone away. We might have to evacuate those rooms that face the Center. Don't know yet," he said, very worried and serious.

I went and stood by the staircase. The lower level of the hotel was an open parking garage. I had to keep people from going down. No one was quite sure if the threat was real but everyone was acting like it was. I was confused but alert. I thought it was probably phony, but at least entertaining. Eventually, I became restless and the place was like a ghost town. Everyone was locked down. No one was moving.

After what seemed a long time, I went down the stairs to peek at the parking lot. I had my sandwich with me, thought a stroll and a bite would be a fine thing to do. The parking lot was a little below ground level. Like a basement. The street and the sidewalk were maybe five feet above and the walls did not go all the way up.

I stepped out and leaned against a wall, about to bite when five or six cops suddenly jumped down from the sidewalk and into the parking garage. "Down, down, down!" one of them shouted, not to me but to the other cops. They landed on the asphalt and crouched on their knees, ducking for cover. Instantly I did the same thing, then duck-hopped back to the stairs.

A small blast went off. The cops had detonated the pipe bomb right outside the hotel. My head exploded at #1: how dumb the cops were and #2: how dumb it would have been for me to take a piece of shrapnel to the head and die in my shitty black pants with the safety pin fly. And #3: I was going to use this adventure to go upstairs and talk for at least an hour on the clock, maybe more.

## Bus Fire

It pays to be a pack rat. Often it is looked down upon, and yeah, there are legitimate mentally ill hoarders out there. I majored in History, so, as a Historian, it is my job to keep all kinds of shit and to have good piles all around me and my living space at all times. Check and check.

All this to say, I have an award certificate from the Holiday Inn that says Rex saved the day when he put out the bus fire. I have a certificate saying I was a hero, and should you think that I should remember this incident, you would be wrong. I have a memory of using a fire extinguisher, yes, but not where I was using it. How many lives did I save? How can I keep track, even? I was probably in shock. Maybe it will come out in therapy one day like so many other, um, great things have.

There was a girl that got hired to do the phones. Clara was a sharp and sassy Latina with high hair-sprayed nineties hair, tight shirts, thong showing (as was popular), and a laugh louder than mine. I made her laugh a lot somehow. I was a goof. I could do impressions of the lame boss and the mutant bellboy boss. One shift I came into the back office and she ripped off her telephone headset, locked the door, and jumped on me. I was shocked as her tongue went in my mouth and my tongue tried to figure out how to be cool. I had made out with three people in my sheltered life. "Grab my tits, c'mon, grab my tits! Oh fuck, I've never been with a white guy!" We made out until someone knocked on the door. We did this thing more than a few times. Once she had me on my back on the office floor and was grinding on top of me. "Oh my god, you are hard, right? I'm gonna grab it. Oh my god! Why are you so cute? My boyfriend will kill you, oh my god. Are you gonna fuck me or what?"

She was in beauty school and drafted me to go in and get my eyebrows waxed. She said it was a must. I went to a tiny salon on 28th and Sandy. Waited around forever for something I didn't want. She finally sat me down. "Oh wow, you came, haha, you must really like me! Okay, let's get this monobrow." She took a popsicle stick and dipped it in the wax. I did not know this was hot wax. I just about screamed. She laughed so hard she had to put her hands on her knees. "Okay, okay, stop, haha. Hold on. Let me get it, I have to pull fast, okay?" She pulled fast and a triangle of skin about the size of a dime tore off my face. My monobrow and all the flesh between my brows a bloody crater. "Woah, I'm bleeding! Clara!" Again, the hands to her knees.

I shut down the next makeout session. Not because of my eyebrows, which made her bust out laughing every time she saw me. "You don't want to fuck me? Lots of guys would die to get this. You know that, right? I would fuck you so good, you have no idea. You think I'm hot, right?" And I did think she was hot. I was a Tarzan of a kid and had no idea or confidence in how to handle a girl like this. I was conflicted and confused and usually said No to everything. So I said we should stop. I also reminded her that she had a boyfriend who she described as a six-foot-tall buff Black gangster. Her feelings were hurt, which I thought strange. I would miss her grabbing and grinding on me in the elevator and rubbing her tits on me. But I didn't want to die.

She was crying in the back a couple weeks later. She had just turned in her resignation. "I'm fucking pregnant. It fucking sucks, Rex. I have to quit beauty school and move back with my Mom. The guy left and I'm not going to get anything, I got dumped and I can't even work here now." She cried and I put my hand on her shoulder and she hugged me hard and close.

When she quit, Morgan said something like, "Aw man, Clara was cool. And hot, wow."

"Yeah, we used to make out back in the office. She grabbed my dick in the elevator!"

"Ha! Yeah right, bellboy! You could never land someone that fine. Haha."

| 1   Wages, tips, other comp. | 2   Federal income tax withheld |
|---|---|
| 7027.12 | 589.03 |
| 3   Social security wages | 4   Social security tax withheld |
| 7027.12 | 435.68 |
| 5   Medicare wages and tips | 6   Medicare tax withheld |
| 7027.12 | 101.89 |

| a   Control Number | Dept. | Corp. | Employer use only |
|---|---|---|---|
| 001103 JGK | 018012 | A | 141 |

c   Employer's name, address, and ZIP code

**GRAND AVENUE HOTEL ASSOC
HOLIDAY INN PTLD DWNTOWN
1111 THIRD AVE STE 3030
SEATTLE WA 98101**

| b   Employer's FED ID number | d   Employee's SSA number |
|---|---|
| 93-1002377 | |
| 7   Social security tips | 8   Allocated tips |
| 9   Advance EIC payment | 10  Dependent care benefits |
| 11  Nonqualified plans | 12  Benefits included in box 1 |
| 13  See Instrs. for box 13 | 14  Other |

| 15  Stat emp. | Deceased | Pension plan | Legal rep. | Hshld. emp. | Deferred comp. |
|---|---|---|---|---|---|
| | | | | | |

e/f   Employee's name, address and ZIP code

**REX MARSHALL
TH #9
PORTLAND,OR 97202**

| 16  State | Employer's state ID | 17  State wages, tips, etc. |
|---|---|---|
| OR | 396973 5 | 7027.12 |
| 18  State income tax | | 19  Locality name |
| 398.67 | | |
| 20  Local wages, tips, etc. | | 21  Local income tax |
| | | |

**Federal Filing Copy**

# W-2 Wage and Tax Statement 1997

OMB No. 1545-0008

Copy B To be filed with employee's Federal Income Tax Return

# FOUNDERS MEMORIAL LIBRARY

NORTHERN ILLINOIS UNIVERSITY, DEKALB, IL

1998

$5.00/HOUR (LOWER MINIMUM WAGE IN THE MIDWEST)

I've always been drawn to the comfort of a library. Every new city I've lived in, the library was at the top of the list to investigate and find a corner to call my own. I relocated to corn country Illinois when I was twenty-three. Around three months went by and I declared that I was the most lonely guy on the planet. I was so bored that I decided to finish college. I had put myself through five years of part-time classes at four different schools, mostly as a hobby. There was no career in mind. I had been alone for a lot of my life, but I learned after a summer in Illinois—where I only knew my late-seventies grandparents—that I needed to break myself apart and create a new Rex. One that was not afraid of that thing called "people." I drafted myself into a job at the Circulation Desk at the Northern Illinois University library. I had avoided front line customer work at every job I had ever had. Now I was charging in. It was time to kill the shy guy.

There was a hippie kid who worked there. Very nice and very much the cliché of a Phish fan. I told him I had just moved to Illinois from Oregon. "What? Why would you come out here! Wow. That's backwards. You were in paradise." I told him I was out here to be close to my grandparents. My great-aunt had died and they offered me her house to move into. Free rent. I had been working since I was eleven and suddenly didn't have to struggle. I didn't have a job for a whole summer. I didn't need one. My grandparents were taking care of me. They paid my bills, paid my classes, and bought me food. I went for this library job because I wanted to learn how to talk to people. To shatter my shell. I didn't need this job. That's the first time in my life I ever had that option. I was free! Goddamn I was losing my mind with the freedom, though. I was very alone. I had to go where the people were.

Professor Kalisnof. One of our regular characters in the library. He was a Professor in the History department. He was a supreme pain. A cliché of a mad bookworm with tousled hair, clothes thrown on without care. Not a nice or polite bone in his body. Really, he was more a mutant than a dick. You could see it wasn't exactly his fault that he was who he was. He wrote a ton of books and was a prize scholar for NIU. Anytime we saw him coming, the quickest and smartest of us library workers would duck and cover.

One day, he came to return some books. You see, the library made professors bring back their books every five years. Profs believe they own any library books they check out. They assume the library is their free pile. So, libraries inevitably make some rules about Professors returning their books once every few years.

To make sure the books still exist. To maybe give a poor student a chance to look at them. Kalisnof must have gotten the call because he squeaked in with an actual grocery cart full of books one day. Not even stacked, just thrown in. He was high-pitched whining about the unfair hassle of it. That's when I got the idea.

I had a shift with Runi, a clever and sneaky Vietnamese girl, and I threw out the idea that we should put a book on hold for him. Something fun for him to pick up. We laughed a ton, teased out the idea. How great it would be to hit him with a book prank. We started looking up titles in the catalog. We brainstormed on subjects until we found an incredible, almost unbelievable book. It was available at another library. We could order it through Interlibrary Loan on his behalf. Runi clicked all the way to the last confirmation screen. We paused there, too afraid to seal the deal. That feeling where you are working up the courage to do something, boiling with anticipation, is a rich one to lather in. We dared each other but were frozen.

Runi suddenly jumped up from a few feet away and slapped the keyboard with her open hand. "Oh, fuck it!" The book title was *ORAL SEX*. The request for *ORAL SEX* was sent for Prof Kalisnof.

Couple weeks later, guess who's working the Circ desk? Runi! I don't think I was there. She told me about it. But I can see it in my head. Maybe I was there? Maybe I wasn't, but wanted to be so badly that I wrote and fabricated the memory. I swear to you I can see the scene. Kalisnof had a dozen or so books to pick up as always. He was loud, being rude. In hindsight, I think he may have been autistic. Or maybe I am being too diplomatic and he was just an asshole. He never treated us well. You don't have to be a doctor to diagnose dick. He was demanding and very specific. Runi went through the stack and pushed them across the counter to him. He always looked at every book and checked to see if we had found the right edition for him. Runi was standing there, pretty nonchalant. I was watching from behind the safety of some bookshelves behind the counter.

Suddenly, very loudly, Kalisnof said, "*ORAL SEX*!! What is this? Where did this come from? Oh! This isn't mine! What is this! *ORAL SEX*, oh no no. No! This isn't mine at all! What is this book??" I don't know how many times he said *ORAL SEX*. It was beautiful. Runi held her laughs in between tight teeth. "Okay, okay, I'm not sure—it says it came from InterLibrary. I can just send it back."

"Oh, well, it's a mistake, I did NOT order *ORAL SEX*! You make sure it's off my account and not checked out to me. I didn't order. Take it off my account now," he snarled.

"Yes, yes, of course. I already took it off and will just send it back."

"How could this happen? I didn't order that."

He said that about ten more times before he huffed out the door.

It was a small, dumb victory but it helped morale. We had put some silly points up on the board and defeated the mad professor. He was such a demanding ass. He was a professor, so we were expected and trained to treat him like royalty. "The Customer is Always Right." I'd first heard that in the retail world. Who could I blame for this workplace mentality? Where workers have to say, Yes, sir, may I have another? Everytime they are yelled at or shit on? I would say watch out to those with that attitude. Those workers may be cooking up something special just for you.

Runi was desperately in love with my friend Emmett Meek. What a name, right? Maybe he will sue me, but I need to use his real name because c'mon. Runi had long legs and smooth skin and was funny and just a package deal. Emmett was embarrassed about how she pined over him. It was as obvious as a billboard. I was a shy one who was trying to quash that trait. I watched Emmett with this girl crushing hard and I couldn't stand it. "What is wrong with you, man? She is incredible and wants you. It's a crime." He hemmed and hawed and basically said he wasn't that into her. Maybe this is a boring story but it had to come out. I dunno. Runi, I hope you found some real funny fucker who treats you how you deserve.

I got arrested later that year and my name was in the school paper in the Crime Report section. I was not used to living in a town of 15k. News travels fast. The newspaper was all over the library and everybody read it. I went to work and my coworkers were waiting to pounce. My boss, Cliff, called me into his office as soon as he heard me punch in.

"Hey, Rex. So I saw your name in the *Northern Star*. I don't know what you and Myron were up to, but looks like you goofed around. I hope you learned a lesson or two. Take care."

Myron worked at the library, too, so it was the Rex and Myron scandal show for the week.

Things escalated fast that night. I started drinking beer when I moved to that town. Something that I hadn't really done much of before. I was afraid of what I might become if I drank. But, I had to make friends in this Midwest bowl of a town so I chugged Schlitz and Hamms and rolled the dice. Would I become a raging alcoholic like my Dad? Let's find out! I joke. Drinking was a heavy decision to make. I knew the statistics. I was afraid. I drank for the first time when I was nineteen, got really sick, and didn't again till I was twenty-three. Anyhoo, I didn't become an alky or too much of an asshole. Ass, yes, but not a fully formed asshole. I went to Myron's apartment one night and one night only to hang. April 19th, 1999. We drank a bunch of beer and a bit of liquor and decided to go run around.

I had recognized the wild streak in Myron. He had a fast-moving brain and was too intense for a lot of people. He had bright blonde hair and a surfer crew cut. His laugh was maniacal. We ended up on campus by the football stadium and found it easy to get into. There was a chain link gate that was padlocked, but we squeezed through and the door to the stadium was open. We strolled through the dark halls feeling sneaky. We laughed and shouted. We went outside on the bleachers and sat and drank. Back in the stadium, someone was in there with a flashlight and said, "Hey! Stop!" and we did the opposite.

Myron said, "Run!" and I didn't hesitate. Long story short, we evaded yelling voices, flashlights, and ran and hid for about three hours. "I think we can just walk out and say sorry, right?" I said. We were crouched somehow in a part of the roof at this point when Myron, fully out of his mind and not okay—and I finally saw, yes, okay, he is fucking intense—said "Okay, they are NOT going to take me. I cannot get arrested. Do you know who my family is? My Dad?! No. I am like a bullet. I am a sharp, unstoppable bullet and they will not get me. I am a bullet and they will not even see me. I'm telling you, Rex. They won't catch me alive."

Myron had gone full-tilt *Apocalypse Now* and I had said I wanted to turn myself in, but after that speech I was fully recruited for the hard bullet escape. We ended up back on the bleachers, and we made it down on the field and ran across and over a fence and I was shocked to see five cop cars and thought I heard a German Shepherd and we hid under some bushes next to the parking lot. There was a posse after us and my pal was full-tilt losing his shit. Now, about my shoes.

I moved from Portland, Oregon to Dekalb, Illinois. I still wear black leather shoes 95% of the time. In 1998 I moved out there in a cardigan and shiny black shoes. I was the only one who looked like that at NIU and the word "faggot" found me in the halls right away. I was called that for most of my high school "journey" and should have been used to it. It was a bummer. I found friends and some of them had nice shoes. Myron had some dumbass sneakers on, but I was the one with the shiny black leather shoes that the cop's flashlight reflected off of, and that was how Rex and Myron got misdemeanor drunk charges.

There were so many cop cars waiting to give us a lift. Don't do shit in a small town because all small town cops are bored and eager. They took us in separate cars. Arriving at the station, they made me take everything out of my pockets and take off my clothes and put on orange sweats and orange sandals. A cop put his whole hand up my ass. Kind of overkill, I thought. These cops watch too many movies. I guess a kid in patent leathers looks like a drug smuggler.

After I pulled up my new orange pants, I was sent out to the waiting room to wait for my appearance in front of the judge. I was spiking with nerves walking in there. Who was going to kick my ass? There were about ten full-grown adult males in orange in that room. I was shaking. I tried not to think about the movie *American Me* starring Edward James Olmos. All gathered around a TV set in the corner. One of them looked up and saw me. Oh shit, I thought. Eye contact. Here it comes.

"Hey man, you hear what happened?" said this tough-looking white guy.

"Uh, no, I just got here..." I said.

"Man, pull up a seat. Somebody shot up this school in Colorado. Killing all those kids. They're still holed up in there, man. The world has gone crazy," he said. He was shook. All the guys had a concerned look. I forgot I was in jail.

I pulled up a chair and watched live TV coverage of the Columbine Massacre. A very long night had warped into a very heavy morning. On the plus side, I had no worries of getting beat up anymore. All of us criminals were glued to that news coverage trying to wrap our brains around this new carnage. Soon, we were all called into a room with bleacher seats and a big-screen TV. The Judge videoed in and we all had our turns with him. He was lenient on Myron and me as this was our first offense, so he let us go without bail. Told us to come back for sentencing. The jail was way out there and I walked back to campus and actually made it to one of my classes. My twenty-four-year-old brain was bruised and reeling. Sitting in a Japanese history class without sleep after being handcuffed, strip-searched, jailed, and released. Watching and failing to digest gruesome history in real time on a tiny black-and-white TV in a county jail.

I talked to Myron once after. "Hey, so wow, my parents didn't find out, thank god. And they never will. Anyway, I can't hang out with you anymore, Rex. I can't be your friend. Crazy stuff happens with me and you together. I just can't."

**Thursday, April 22, 1999**

# Newsetc... 2

## IllinoisLottery

Tickets for Wednesday, April 21, 1999

EST BIG GAME LOTTO JACKPOT - $16 MILLION

EST LOTTO JACKPOT - $2 MILLION

### Midday

| PICK 3 | PICK 4 |
|---|---|
| 4 1 4 | 8 7 6 9 |

### Evening

| PICK 3 | PICK 4 |
|---|---|
| 9 8 2 | 3 5 6 1 |

*...celebrating 100 years*

## On this day in NIU history...

April 22, 1986

Members of the Illinois state legislature may have begun investigating the nearly $100,000 spent by NIU for renovation, remodeling and refurnishing of NIU President Clyde Wingfield's university-owned home at 901 Woodlawn Dr.

In a year and a half, NIU employees spent more than 2,600 hours working on the president's home. Labor and material costs to the NIU Physical Plant for remodeling and renovation of the building exceeded $63,000.

In addition to this figure, about $26,000 was spent by NIU for furnishings and about $10,000 was paid to outside contractors for materials and services performed.

NorthernStar

## NorthernStar

### Managers, editors and advisers

| | |
|---|---|
| Editor in chief (753-0100) | Jim Menned |
| Managing editor (753-0117) | Bill Tynan |
| Editorial editor (753-9642) | Josh Gaby |
| Campus editor (753-9643) | Iva-Marie Palmer |
| Asst. campus editor | Katie Scrivaho |
| City editor (753-9644) | Joe Biesk |
| Asst. city editor | Justin Hoffman |
| Sports editor (753-9640) | Stacy Clardie |
| Asst. sports editor | Brian Schlumburg |
| Features editor | Liz Vivanco |
| Weekender editor (753-9639) | Kara Pipitone |
| Asst. Weekender editor | Eric Clark |
| Photo editor (753-1602) | Sandy Coley |
| News photo editor | Sam Summers |
| Features photo editor | Nate Whinnery |
| AP wire editor | Idon Pang |
| Copy desk chief (753-9646) | Jana Thompson |
| Asst. copy desk chief | Kasey Baker |

## PoliceBeat

*The following was taken directly from the DeKalb Fire Department, DeKalb Police, University Police records, DeKalb County Sheriff's reports and DeKalb County Court records.*

- Katherine Colpen, 18, 501 Spring Ave., was arrested at about 8:20 p.m. Tuesday on a warrant for alleged consumption of alcohol as a minor. She was released on $1,000 bond.

- A complainant at Jo-Ann Fabrics, 1712 Sycamore Rd., reported to police that a man came into the business at about 4 p.m. Tuesday and made a purchase with a suspected counterfeit bill. Police checked the bill and found it was counterfeit. Police have no suspects.

- Kenneth H. Williams, Chicago, was arrested by University Police at about 2:30 a.m. Tuesday and charged with obstruction of justice and driving with a suspended license on Stadium Drive East. He was taken to the DeKalb Police station where he posted bond.

- ___________, 1400 W. Lincoln, and Rex K. Marshall, of Ottawa, were arrested by UP at about 3 a.m. Monday and charged with criminal trespass to Huskie Stadium. They were taken to the DeKalb Police Department and have pending bonds.

# Carnegie Mellon University Engineering Library



I graduated with a BA in History and a minor in Philosophy. Rather than waltz into the seven-figure job I knew must await a fella with a History degree, I moved to Pittsburgh to follow my girlfriend, who'd gotten accepted to a PhD program at Penn State. I landed another library job. I was thrilled to continue my library path. I was thrilled that full time at Carnegie Mellon was thirty-five hours a week. I was making solid cash. My first salary job. A beautiful campus populated with beautiful rich kids. I was twenty-five and felt forty. I am not and never was a higher-ed enthusiast, but I have been working in them for over thirty years at this point. It's complicated.

I worked so many grueling jobs before I went to college full time. College to me was an escape from the grindstone. I did the assignments; popped the quizzes; turned work in and then forgot about whatever I'd learned, or not. What a dream. By the time I finished college at NIU, I felt like an old vet. Most of my classmates were

"

years younger than me, talking about the future they would shape. They were sweet, naive fools. I was in the Marxist History group. So many rebels in the cornfields of Illinois, talking how different their futures would be.  I knew full well that when I graduated I would be back out there, not a rebel, not a world-changer, just a working-class slob gatherer of cash. In the trenches broken by money, as we all are bound to be.

I wasn't that much older than most of the student body at CMU, but I was out of my class and out of place. I wanted to make friends and make music but found it impossible. I had a cheap one-bedroom in a big old house on Squirrel Hill. Jerry's Records was right down the hill. My girlfriend was immersed in her new program and had a stunning marble-floored apartment in a gorgeous apartment building. I was soon outclassed and out of place with my own girlfriend. She brought me to her "colleague's" house and they talked about Derrida and Foucault and Marx, and though I knew and had read those people they did not look at me as a peer. PhDs gotta stick together, I guess. I felt like shit and she went with her new people and I was alone in the unfriendly Midwestern  but more old-world—cold. The most cold I have ever been was in that city of Pittsburgh.

You know what? I had no crazy stories at this library. I was there maybe eleven months. I didn't do much of anything at this job. It blew my mind. I had it made, making fine money. Healthcare, pension, vacation days. I was flush with money. I really didn't have shit to do 90% of the time. I shared an office with the library secretary. She laughed at everything. We got drinks once and even danced for a couple songs. She was married, happily so. She talked a lot about a friend of hers who had just died. She really loved the guy. She cried in the office a while after. I had no frame of reference and just tried to think of crazy shit to say. To get her to laugh. Best I could do.

When I was first being shown around, the boss of Circulation was Nancy, a big old gal with a fine guffaw and a lot of insecurities. She asked, "What are you?" and I said, "Uh, what?" She repeated, "What are you? You know? Where are ya from?" And I said, "I mean, I'm from Vegas. My grandparents are out in Illinois. My great-grandma moved there from Poland." "Ah! You're a Pole! Me too! Mary, oh she's Eyetalian, oh well, but yeah, we got a couple other Poles, I'll introduce you." I had never had this Old World vetting before. We don't do that in the Southwest. Or West, for that matter.

I was at CMU for less than a year. Nancy tried to talk me out of quitting. So did the head of the library, Lyne. A name I've always loved. She said there were so many opportunities at CMU. For someone as young as me. I had a lot to gain from sticking with it. It was sweet and helped my stunted esteem, but I was already gone.

One of my last days there, I brought an acoustic guitar and sang a song I wrote about the Sorrel Engineering Library. Part of my continuing effort to get rid of the shy guy.

> *Library, Library, don't ever change*
> *Library, Library, don't ever change*
> *Something something something something*
> *But that I-L-L woman is mighty strange!*
> *Library, Library, don't ever change*

The InterLibrary Loan person was a Black woman who was on the same level as me as far as teasing and clowning. I knew she could take a jab. I put everybody's name in that song and watched them light up. They brought cake and snacks and everyone laughed at my song. I liked those folks a lot, and like most of those jobs I left, I never saw these coworkers again.

I left the coldest city I had ever been to and made the slow, weird choice to move back to Portland. I rented a Penske truck and put my now-substantial belongings in. I drove from Chicago and made it all the way to BLAH BLAH Montana without stopping. Thirty-two hours straight. This has nothing to do with jobs, I know, but c'mon. I drove for thirty-two goddamn hours. Without coffee or caffeine 'cause I knew that makes you piss and the crash when it wears off is no good. No drugs, just willpower 'cause I wanted to get this move in the bag. I wanted to start my life again. I wanted to get another library job and make music on the side.

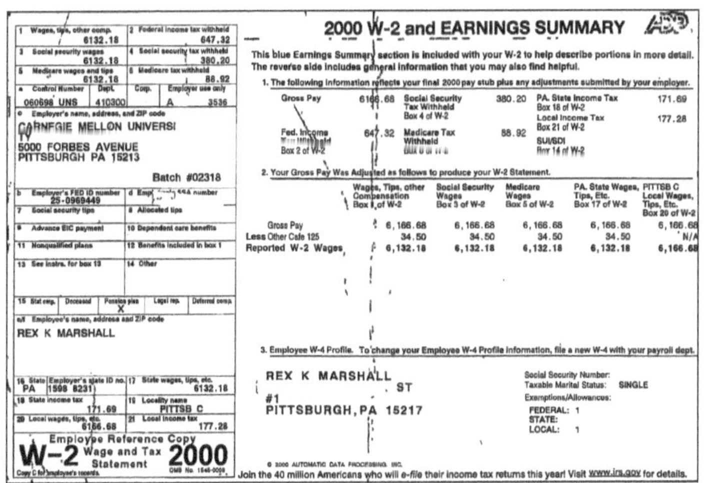

# U Store Self Storage



So, my glorious return to Portland and I wound up working at a storage place. Welcome to the Depression Zone, Where the Customer Is Always Sad. That should have been the vinyl banner hanging above the entrance to the U-Store Self Storage on 28th and Sandy. There is nothing but grief and sad transitional phases to be found at any self-storage place. This U-Store used to be an old furniture factory in the 1890s. Was converted into a self-storage thing in the eighties. Half of the building was old growth beams, thick and cracked. Every ancient floor creaked and sagged with each footstep. The shorter building was Leaning-Tower-of-Pisa-slanted and rumored to be very much not in code. Also maybe haunted. Some units constantly leaked when it rained hard. Others had rats.

The self-storage job turned out to be the most down-and-out soul-sucking job I've ever had. The other jobs were not glamorous, but couldn't hold a candle to the rich sediment of desperation and skid-row spiraling that a storage place represents. Who uses storage places? Maybe you think of college kids, or families with too much adventure gear. Maybe a hoarding husband is shamed by his orderly wife into renting an extra room. A grampa with too much fishing gear. A couple who moves in together to save some dough, but have to get a unit as they don't have time to consolidate all their belongings.

What you come to find out by working at one of these places is that a fair amount of storage stories involve death, eviction, nasty divorces, breakups, unemployment, homelessness, addictions of all kinds, and those desperate in-between places we find ourselves when on the icy sidewalk of change.

I remember a family that had just survived a house fire. Insurance was paying for a hotel until they could lock down their settlement. They were able to salvage some things from the house, and had to put them somewhere. I couldn't count the number of evictions where people were out on their ass and needed a quick solution for all their stuff. Divorces aplenty came through. Put your failed marriage in this 8x12! A man chain-smoking and scrambling, cramming what's left of his life into a 10x10 unit. He doesn't even have everything boxed. Hiding shit from the ex so she doesn't get it in the divorce. The garbage bag is luggage for many of these types. Hiding things from the lawyers. Piles of shirts still on hangers just thrown on a flatbed. I would see these people unloading their things and it was 80% worthless detritus. Particle board furnishings from Target. Walmart BBQs and Costco detergent. Boxes of *National Geographic*. The smaller units went for about sixty a month. Which isn't a lot, unless you consider the twenty dollars worth of crap you are paying to store. We are bound to our possessions. They demand our money and attention.

If a person stopped paying, they were given several warnings that their stuff would be forfeited and sold. The laws are strict on this one. Once the red tape time period had passed, the U-Store could cut the lock off and auction the units. An ad had to be put in the classifieds to make a public statement about the auctioning of unpaid units. A renter had up until the day before an auction to come in and make arrangements to keep their things. Often they would come in and beg. My slothy managers had to earn their money those days. I felt parts of my soul die as I listened. "Man, that's all my stuff. All my photo books and tools. My kids' toys!"

"Yes, Carl, that was your stuff, but if you don't pay us one-hundred and fifty dollars today by six p.m. it's not yours anymore."

"Well, I'm just gonna come in and buy my stuff back at your fucking auction!"

"You know you can't do that, Carl."

"But it's my stuff! All my stuff!"

All the words in the world mean nothing without money.

Auction day was full of sleaze. Greasy vultures swarmed in to pick over the lost lives. It was a god-awful day to have to work. I wished I had a firehose to blast full throttle in the faces of these leeches. Auction folks got to peek inside the to-be-auctioned unit for about five minutes. No touching, no looking through boxes or suitcases. A quick peek. Sight unseen for the most part. One of my managers would start the auction. These bidders thought they were big shots with their fifty-dollar bids. Most units sold for only a few hundred dollars. Once you win an auction you have two days to clean it out. Naturally, they would flaunt their treasures. "There was a '62 Harley behind that mattress, haha!" or "Think I'll keep most of the guns I found in 32A." I wished one of these parasites would find a dead body in a suitcase just once. Or a jar full of bubonic plague.

Weekends I worked at the NW location all by my solo self. Opened and closed the place without company. It was the best day of my work week. I listened to *Car Talk* on a dusty boombox. Read a stack of paperbacks. Slow-walked endlessly around the maze of units. There was a ladder there and a manager showed me how they used it to look into the units. None of them had roofs! They were basically wooden cubicles built inside a warehouse. I heard recycled myths passed around of people trying to secretly live in their storage units. Maybe that's why we had ladders.

Every weekend as I was closing, I would see a guy rush out right before I slammed and locked the garage door. He wore a hat and was so inconspicuous that he was conspicuous. I never saw him come in, only when he quickly ran out. I guessed that he was coming from the B section, which was to the left of my office. All the units over there were rented, so it was hard to narrow down which one was his. As I stumbled around bored on a shift, I noticed that one of the doors was closed but not padlocked. I saw the guy run out as I went to put up the Closed sign. I went back to the section and the padlock was back on that door. B12. Gotcha.

I locked all the doors and flipped the Closed sign over, then rushed for the ladder. I had no guesses as to what I would find in there. Really couldn't imagine. I climbed to the top and peeped over the wall. It was one of those moments where you feel your mind trying to take it all in and your astonishment is just overloading the system. It was a 5x10 rectangular unit. I was looking over an eight-foot wall down onto a sloping hill of porn. The magazines at the highest point of the pile in back were about five feet up the wall. They were by no means stacked in orderly piles. Near the door was a folding chair by a milk crate that acted as a table. On the crate was a stack of porn and a roll of paper towels. There were a few stacked paperbacks against the wall, which I suppose were porn novels. The guy sat in his chair and when done with a magazine he chucked it onto the breaking tsunami wave mountain of paper porn.

I looked up the unit's history when I went back to the office. The account had an illegible name scrawled in awful handwriting. This one had been rented before the company had computers. It was on an automatic payment system. That had been set up at least seven years before. Because he was on autopay, he got the sixty dollars a month deal. He had sat on his folding chair and been throwing pornos at the wall for probably a decade.

I didn't want to be a narc. I never told management about my private eye work. I thought the porn unit and its decade-old porn hill pretty freaky, but nothing too crazy. I grew up in Vegas, so maybe I have a higher tolerance for smut. Was it deviant or was this just a guy finding some alone time? I'm not saying I ever wanted to strike up a conversation with that man. But I also didn't want to ruin what could have been his only escape.

This was the one and only period in my life where I lived in a house with a bunch of people. Four of us under one roof. At one point six, when we took in a couple who had just moved from Baltimore. One night we had a party and I drank every drink imaginable and entertained myself for sure. I was on the roof at one point, yelling at the night sky and laughing my ass off.

That morning I had to wake at eight and be at the U Store by nine. As I walked out the door I grabbed a plastic trash bag. I knew I would need it. I felt like my veins were pure booze just pumping warm, cheap booze. I got there, opened the big garage door and the front door, grabbed the cordless phone, and ran for the bathroom. I puked hard and good, and black bile poured out. I went back to the office, checked for vacant units, and picked the closest one to the office. Again with the cordless phone in my hand, I unlocked that unit, went in, shut the door, and laid down on the concrete and died. The phone ringing Lazarused me and I remembered where I was. "U Store NorthWest," I said.

"Yeah hi, I'm at your office, is anyone working?"

"I will send someone right there," I said. I stood up on wobbly legs and patted down my hair. I signed up someone for a new unit in record time. I got all the signatures and a check and even managed to lock it in the cash register before I ran off and puked again.

Especially after that day, I was determined to get back into the comfy world of libraries. I applied to them the whole time I worked at the U Store. I finally got a bite and had a strange interview where I mainly talked about where I had lived, the fact that my name means King in Latin, and where my parents were from. I did not get a call back. I waited a week till I picked up the phone. I said, "Hello, can I speak with Philip? Tell him it's Rex."

"Hey, this is Philip. Oh, hi Rex. What's up?"

"Hi, I was checking in on the position. I interviewed last week. Sorry if I'm bothering you, it's been a week and I just wanted to follow up."

"Oh, right, yeah, you got the job. Come in whenever you want to start. Okay, we'll see you, bye-bye!" and Philip hung up the phone.

I trusted this unusual job offer and was over the moon. I put in notice at the U Store. I typed out a letter on my electric typewriter and found a clean envelope. I handed it to the Assistant Manager and he was bummed. Caught me off guard a bit. He seemed genuinely sad. Later in the day, he found me. "They want to talk to you in the office. Let's walk over there now." The boss of the place was a dead ringer for Wilford Brimley. Hair but balding, with the glasses and gruffness. A guy of few words and you had better listen close to those few words.

"So, we would hate to see you go, Rex. You're a good kid. Someone with a college degree like you could go far in this company. And we are only growing. There's a lot of opportunity here for a ton of advancement. I will teach you everything I know. I could see you as a real manager someday. Maybe at the top. Here's what we can offer you right now in terms of salary and benefits. Let me know by the end of the week."

He said some numbers I can't remember but I remember they were fine numbers. He had dumped a career in my lap. I could become the storage king. I could rule over the belongings of the dispossessed masses. I could be grand auctioneer to the toothless vultures who swooped down when unpaid units went under the hammer. I could hire workers, pay them minimum wage, and make them wear tap dance shoes and pink polos.

As he was pitching my new life to me, the voice in my head clearly and with great enunciation said NO. Sometimes I can wrestle with the voice and make deals or bargains. This was not one of those times. This was a NO from my bones. It was flattering to be seen as valuable, as someone they wanted to keep. It was interesting/weird how much my college degree meant to them. The boss and the assistant manager did not have college degrees themselves, and looked at me as kind of a golden child. I couldn't tell them that college for me was mostly a way to escape from jobs. I didn't go to college so I could then get a job. I went to college to get away from all the goddamn jobs.

I said some words of gratitude and declined the offer as gently as I could. Wilfred was let down for sure. "Think about it," he said. I shook his hand. My paper-thin ego had received a rare boost and I was truly proud to have been considered. While at the same time I was thinking, oh no, guys, I could never chuck my life into this work pit. I did not break it to them, but they lived in a fantastically depressing world. Broken lives and all the drama and detritus that comes with that. The storage world of smashed dreams and taking people's belongings if they fucked up. I am going back to the promised land of the library. I want to give away books and pencils, not repo people's lives. I want to have long coffee breaks, read magazines and eat burritos on the front steps of the peaceful, hope-filled, no-retail, noncommercial money blackhole piled high with books, VHS, DVDs, microfiche, and hope.

That brings me to my current job at the PSU Library, which I sauntered into after breaking up with the U Store in 2002. Twenty-four years at one place, lord how did he do it? Maybe this one job deserves its own book, a modest book called *Library*. Maybe I will keep my golden handcuffs on till I hit that pension. I think I qualify in six years. Which was unimaginable when I was hired on.

Back then, I looked at the staff that had been there since the seventies. How does a person do it? My Grampa at Owens Glass for forty-one years. And me somehow. What a traditional old-school worker I've warped into. All the folks who partied and toured in bands in their twenties and thirties, who I envied as they chased their dreams without worry over security or stability. All those rockers are jealous of me now. No one gets healthcare, saves money, buys a house and gets a goddamn pension anymore. I stuck with the safe and predictable life of the full-time job. Even so, maybe I'll drop dead the minute I retire. That would be a fantastic, tragic ending for a book. Maybe not a great ending for a life. If I die soon after being free from all the work I never wanted, I will be truly very upset. You will hear my screams echo loudly from that break room in hell.

# ACKNOWLEDGMENTS

I have never been a part of a fundraiser for my work before. Historically I pay for my own art by getting side jobs or selling prized bric-a-brac. I thought this funder would fail. Massive thanks to all the friends, fans and freaks who clocked in and got us here. 152 people, most of whom I don't know. No refunds!

Thanks to Michelle Kicherer the Boss Banana for eyeballing this and saying yes to publishing. I finally found a driven person who I trust. All your hard work is appreciated!

I need to give a handshake to Brian Alfrey, a true mensch and friend. A real patron of the arts who nurtures and creates culture and community. Keys Lounge is the best bar in Portland. Brian said we can do a book event there. He has no idea what he's agreed to. I hope they have good insurance.

Thanks to Rebekah for being in my life. A kind and generous partner. I finally found someone who understands how much alone time I need to feel normal. She is also a great reader. Sometimes we read books together. What a gem. I wish I could help her quit her job.

Thanks to Gwen Schulte for proofreading and design of this book. Justin Gradin for cover art. Check out his books at Fantagraphics, he is the real deal.

Thanks most of all to Rex Marshall. Rex always wanted to be an author, but had no confidence or guidance. This did not stop him from writing every day, even if only 15 minutes in a break room on a tiny spiral-bound notepad. Those scraps of paper in a forgotten coat pocket do add up. Rex never gave up on writing and here he is with his name on the spine of a book. Something he dreamed about as a kid. Rex still punches a timeclock and has to report to places he would rather not. Still, Rex is grateful that Rex has always carved out time for his art and will leave some cool things behind when he clocks out for good. Thank you. Rex.

Note: All photos included in this book are of actual timestubs, W2s, newspapers, schedules and nametags I held onto for over three decades. Isn't that fucking nuts? Who does that? Shouldn't I get a Nobel or some medal? I call myself a historian but packrat is fine, too.

# READING LIST

*WORKING: PEOPLE TALK ABOUT WHAT THEY DO ALL DAY AND HOW THEY FEEL ABOUT IT* BY STUDS TERKEL. Please read Studs Terkel you fools. I hate that he's so forgotten. Incredible oral historian.

*FACTOTUM* BY CHARLES BUKOWSKI. Wish I could steal that title. Read this and *Post Office*.

*NICKEL AND DIMED: ON (NOT) GETTING BY IN AMERICA* BY BARBARA EHRENREICH. Undercover from the trenches. Spoiler: work sucks.

And read some Karl Marx. Ok not *The Manifesto*, but the stuff about rich people exploiting you.

# WORK SONGS PLAYLIST

"Working on a Coal Mine" –Devo version is great. Lee Dorsey's O.G. is better.

"Working For the Man" –Roy Orbison

"Big Boss Man" –Jimmy Reed

"Working Man Blues" –Merle Haggard

"Sixteen Tons" –Tennessee Ernie Ford

"Talking Hard Work" –Woody Guthrie

"It's a Sin to Be Rich, It's a Low Down Shame to Be Poor" –Lightnin' Hopkins

"Maggie's Farm" –Bob Dylan

"I Wanna Job" –Abner Jay (Folk Song Stylist version)

"House Rent Boogie" –John Lee Hooker

"Working Class Hero" –John Lennon

"Take This Job and Shove It" –Johnny Paycheck

"9 to 5" –Dolly Parton

"We Gotta Get Outta This Place" –The Animals

"Wooden Shoe" –Mattress

**REX MARSHALL** IS FROM LAS VEGAS AND STILL RECOVERING FROM THAT FACT. WHEN HE IS NOT TRADING HIS HOURS FOR MONEY, REX MARSHALL JETS AROUND WITH HIS LONG-RUNNING MUSIC PROJECT, MATTRESS. HE RUNS A SMALL PRINT PUBLICATION CALLED *MERCY FLUSH*. PLAYS VINYL RECORDS IN THE COOLEST BARS. COLLECTS BOOKS, VHS, RECORDS, COINS, SCORPIONS, ROCKS, AND DRUM MACHINES. HIS FAVORITE COLOR USED TO BE BLUE BUT HE DOESN'T PLAY FAVORITES ANYMORE. HE LAUGHS TOO LOUD AND IF YOU MUST, HE PREFERS TEQUILA SODA IN A TALL GLASS.